Up in Nipigon Country

Up in Nipigon Country

Anthropology as a Personal Experience

Edward J. Hedican

Fernwood Publishing • Halifax

To Richard Salisbury (1926–1989)

Editing: Brenda Conroy
Cover art: Shaun Hedican
Design and production: Beverley Rach
Printed and bound in Canada by: Hignell Printing Limited

A publication of:
Fernwood Publishing
Box 9409, Station A
Halifax, Nova Scotia
B3K 5S3

Fernwood Publishing Company Limited gratefully acknowledges the financial support of the Department of Canadian Heritage and the Canada Council for the Arts for our publishing program.

Le Conseil des Arts | The Canada Council
du Canada | for the Arts

Canadian Cataloguing in Publication Data

Hedican, Edward J.
Up in Nipigon country: anthropology as a personal experience

Includes bibliographical references.
ISN 1-55266-046-X

1. Anthropology—Ontario—Nipigon, Lake, Region—Field work. 2. Indians of North America—Ontario—Nipigon, Lake, Region. I. Title.

E78.O5H42 2001   306'.0723   C00-901777-1

Contents

Preface

The unexamined life is not worth living. —Socrates

How important is experience in the fieldwork of social anthropology? The short answer is "probably quite important." But, curiously, anthropologists do not talk about their experiences in the field in a very systematic way, that is, in terms of the role of those experiences in the analysis of their research. When they do approach the subject, it is more anecdotal than analytical. This book is an exploration of my fieldwork experiences among the Ojibwa people of northern Ontario. Its purpose is to illustrate a central point—that a fieldworker's personal experiences play not only a crucial role in what happens in the field, but in the wider contribution that anthropology's qualitative methods make to social science.

It has now been over twenty years since my first anthropological field trip into the Lake Nipigon region of northwestern Ontario. In the intervening years I have written a few journal articles relating to that trip (see Hedican, various dates) and an ethnography (Hedican 1986a). I have also published a general work on Aboriginal people in Canada (Hedican 1995). Yet, despite these works, the job still did not seem complete. Just about every time I had a few spare moments, my mind would drift back to my fieldwork experiences, and I would see the faces of people, hear the sound of wind in the jack pine forest or the laughter of children, or smell the woodstove in my small cabin. My mind is forever replaying the events, sights and sounds of these earlier years.

But I need "freedom between my ears," so this book is partly an attempt to exorcize these images of the past, to resolve the issues they pose, to come to grips with their essential reality—to lay them to rest so I can move on as a scholar and as a human being.

This book had its beginnings in a long car ride with my friend and colleague Stan Barrett. We had just attended the annual meeting of the Canadian Anthropology Society in Calgary, and we decided to visit his brother in Edmonton for the weekend. During the drive, Stan commented that I should write something about my fieldwork experiences in northern Ontario, and we tossed around different ideas and approaches. Would such a work, for example, focus primarily on the various facets of conducting anthropology in the northern subarctic forest, as a means of contributing in some way to the history of anthropology in Canada? We also discussed the possibility of setting the work in a wider context—something that would explore the theoretical and philosophical dimensions of fieldwork. I must admit that I had difficulty in deciding which direction to take. On the one hand, a theoretical discussion of fieldwork would be more difficult than a straightforward rendition of fieldwork events or situations. On the other hand, a more philosophical and theoretical discussion of fieldwork stood to make a greater contribution to the discipline of anthropology. Most books that had come out in recent years on fieldwork accentuated the adventurous side of anthropology—time spent in the mysterious rain forests of Highland New Guinea, a journey through the Amazon jungle, life on a tropical island and the like. Works which explored the deeper meanings of qualitative research were almost non-existent.

I set some of the ideas that Stan and I had talked about down in a paper entitled "The Epistemological Implications of Fieldwork" (1994). The writing of this piece was a difficult task, in a conceptual sense. For example, did I choose a series of fieldwork incidences and then write about their deeper meaning or significance as far as the methodological aspects of anthropology were concerned? Or, did I start out with some general issues in the area of qualitative research and then discuss these in the context of my own fieldwork experience among the Aboriginal peoples of northern Ontario?

Eventually I did hammer out this paper with much help from Andrew Lyons, the editor of *Anthropologica*, where it was published. While this was going on, I began to recount on my computer interesting incidents, situations, people and so on from my fieldwork "up in Nipigon country," north of Thunder Bay. This was done with no particular purpose or overall plan in mind. I realized that somewhere down the road I would have to bring this stream of consciousness in line with some sort of theme or pattern in order to make the work at least partly coherent. It was during my struggles over coherence and unity that I realized a rather obvious fact—what I was attempting to do was what anyone who has ever conducted fieldwork has to do at some point, which is to say, draw out the commonalities of their day-to-day field experiences and organize these according to general themes and issues. However, most fieldworkers probably don't give much conscious thought to the whole process by which they arrive at these themes. Fieldworkers need to develop a higher level of consciousness, an ability to think in areas of abstraction far removed from the goings on at ground level. This process involves interpretive efforts that will not necessarily result in the same conclusions for anyone else doing the same task. So we arrive at the phenomenological-positivist debate about how we interpret what goes on in the world around us and whether there are concrete realities or just ways of experiencing these realities.

In sum, the central focus of this book is on the role of an ethnographer's personal experiences in fieldwork. In particular, I explore issues relating to the meaning of experience, its epistemological status and its place in fieldwork. Granted, much of this discussion concerning experiences in the field makes a contribution by emphasizing what we all have implicitly regarded as important. Yet, I am not aware of another work in anthropology that deals in any direct sense with how an anthropologist's personal experience contributes to the way an ethnography is conducted, especially in terms of the relationship between fieldwork and memory, the fragmentary nature of experience and the cumulative effect of these on the anthropologist's mind. Let us bring what goes on in the field back to centre stage in anthropology and, as in my case here, let us focus on the manner in which the experience of events in the field become transformed into the final product—the ethnographic monograph. To the extent that this task also involves a more profound understanding of one's own life as well, I'm sure Socrates would approve.

Chapter One

Fieldwork in Anthropology

Experience is not what happens to a man. It is what a man does with what happens to him. —Aldous Huxley (1932)

Constructing Ethnographies

The main theme of this book is that fieldwork in anthropology is mainly about the personal experiences of the ethnographer. There has been some discussion in the anthropological literature in recent years about the "hermeneutic" nature of ethnography, about ethnography as a form of writing. This raises some interesting epistemological questions concerning the status of fieldwork. There are those who see fieldwork as an opportunity to apply certain literary devices to describe the people and their behaviour in particular cultures. For these anthropologists the doing of ethnography is not so much the task of documenting some objective, concrete reality as it is the development of an "insider's" perspective of the social and cultural milieu in which people live.

The idea of ethnography as not much more that a literary text might lead one to miss a central point: the writing of an ethnography comes only after many particular events and situations—the ethnographer's accumulated experience. It is these personal experiences that are the building blocks that lead to the field report the anthropologist eventually writes. An examination of these experiences and the role they play in the construction of an ethnography should therefore be significant in the epistemological and methodological enterprise that we call anthropology.

A crucial point is that anthropologists interested in such epistemological questions should consider the status of fieldwork primarily in terms of its experiencial aspects. For example, one of my suggestions is that fieldwork depends quite often on memory constraints, that is, on the way our memories develop over time and in a certain dialectic with our written field notes. The implications of my own ideas on memory and on the fragmentary nature of experience, as well as on their cumulative effect on the anthropologist's mind, are central to this book.

It is an enormous omission that anthropologists do not consider the various ways that our initial experience of events become worked into the final product of the well-articulated ethnography. There is a certain magic in all of this, a slight of hand if you will, that goes unquestioned. We are left to wonder how these neat little packages of "economy," "family," "religion" and so on emerge

out of the seeming hodge-podge of everyday behaviour. Obviously the anthropologist must have spent a lot of time selecting some events for emphasis, while
virtually ignoring others, while never informing readers about these selective
processes. Perhaps this is asking too much of the fieldworker, who may not be
entirely capable of this monumental task.

Just think about it. There is this steady stream of everyday events and
situations that we only get to experience once, from the position that we are in,
at that particular time and place. There could be a thousand different ways we
could perceiving each event, if only we could change our perspective around,
spatially and temporally. We can't do that though, so we are stuck with the first,
and only, run of the picture. We jot down what we see, or think we see, hardly
giving any attention to the various other factors that have led or contributed
to our being at that particular place or point in time. Added to all of this, from
that moment on, we replay in our minds our perceptions about what went on,
trying to make sense of them from various angles and points of view. We can
never be sure what was actually "real" in the first place.

If the making of an ethnography now begins to seem like an impossible task
or at least one not filled with a great deal of honesty, that could be right, but does
that then justify throwing anthropology onto the garbage heap of anachronistic
disciplines, like phrenology or alchemy? I think not; yet it is evident that much
more time should be devoted to what actually goes on in fieldwork. My purpose,
then, is not simply to entertain the reader with humorous, tragic or otherwise
personal experiences of fieldwork but to use various episodes in this stream of
experience as examples of the way an ethnography is constructed—what
Robert Lowie once referred to as "that planless hodge-podge, that thing of
shreds and patches" (1961: 441).

Reflexive Understandings

Much of this book is concerned with what could be called "reflexive
understandings" in fieldwork. Webster's dictionary defines reflexive as "directed or turned back upon itself; introspective." In the context of fieldwork
in anthropology reflexive refers to the ways in which our understandings
accumulate and are transformed in the context of our continued social interaction with the people in our field of study. I must confess I find this process of
organizing our thoughts, putting them down on paper, rethinking them in the
context of subsequent events and situations and then drawing conclusions in
the form of our final ethnographic account to be exceedingly complicated.
Most of us, I suspect, give little thought to what is going on or take little time
to study the various mechanisms of thought that lead to our finally commit-
ting our account to paper. Yet I would contend that understanding this process
of ethnographic reconstruction is necessary in learning about the way we
accomplish our task as fieldworkers. It would be a strange carpenter, doctor or
engineer, for example, who could not tell you in precise detail the step-by-step

processes by which they go about their work and thereby accomplish the ends they desire to achieve.

On the other hand, there are those who would argue that this step-by-step approach is more akin to science, whereas anthropology to them is more of an art, a humanistic endeavour, in which there is little that is absolute or concrete. My purpose here is not to suggest that anthropologists really don't know what they are talking about or that they accomplish their task of ethnographic writing by some slight of hand. Nor am I suggesting that there is something dishonest about the way the experiences involved in conducting a field study find their way into the printed work. In fact, the ability to perform the task at all, to transform the nebulous currents of social behaviour into a comprehensible stream of understanding would appear to be a minor miracle in itself. Yet we still have not devoted enough attention to the process of transforming reflexive understandings into ethnographic generalities. There is much in between these two poles that is presently hidden from us, that is beyond our close scrutiny.

There are those anthropologists who might be excused for feeling that fieldwork does not always leave them full of knowledge but maybe only a little less ignorant. Fieldwork might be likened to a knock on the side of the head. Our view of the world becomes altered in some fundamental way that is difficult to describe or articulate. We might try to bury our apprehensions about what we have gone through, but we nonetheless realize that our experiences have left our view of the world a bit off centre. Our vision is somehow permanently askew, so that we are much less trusting that our previous, comfortably held perceptions can act as a reliable guide. We now tend to look at the world somewhat obliquely, wondering all along whether that particular reality open to us at that particular moment in time might skip a notch. It is like chasing a ball through the air in the summertime when all of a sudden our eyes make direct contact with the sun's brilliance. Startled and dazed, we stumble about, trying to figure out where we are and what has happened.

Fieldwork also has a habit of leaving a permanent record of discontinuous events in our subconscious that keep bubbling to the surface whenever we let our guard down. We could be shaving or driving to work when all of a sudden there is a direct recall of some event or situation which happened years ago, that now, for some unknown reason, requires a thorough thinking through. Of course we cannot give it the attention it needs and so, as with a cranky child in the supermarket, we tell it to be quiet for the time being and otherwise try to muddle our way along. A curious thing about these flashbacks of fieldwork situations: they are not the pressing concerns we had when we were actually conducting the fieldwork: rather, they are the events that we did not pay a lot of attention to at the time because they did not seem that important.

Is this the price that anthropologists have to pay for doing fieldwork? If it is, then it is a heavy burden to bear. We work not only as forlorn "strangers in a strange land" but are left as strangers unto ourselves. Anthropologists are thought to be the oddballs of the social sciences and at times might even play up to these perceptions, donned in safari hat and khaki shorts, but what is more important than these outward appearances is what goes on under the anthropologist's pith helmet.

Fieldwork in a Log Cabin Village

Here is an example of the sort of situation that is encountered by the fieldworker. The scene is a log-cabin village of Ojibwa in the far reaches of northern Ontario (see "Collins" on the map). There are no cars or roads or televisions here in Collins—just the people and the all-encompassing jack pine forest. In my cabin I have a small desk and chair in one corner, accompanied by an over-turned garbage can with a pillow on top which serves as a seat for my visitors. There is also a bench near the door so that people who happened to feel a bit nervous at first about visiting could keep their distance. Most everyone eventually moved over beside the desk because the candles and coal oil lamp made it hard to see even at twelve feet (the length of the cabin). The can beside the desk left us "cheek by jowl," and the people would bend closer when they thought they had something important to say.

This cabin was the place where I gathered much of the information about village life, as just about everyone showed up beside the desk at one time or another, often spending long hours recounting their memories, perceptions, frustrations and insights. At the time, it all seemed a jumble of fieldwork, entertainment and relaxation to fill in the long winter evenings. Late at night the flickering lamp made the shadows and shapes flow back and forth as if they were liquid. On one occasion, a middle-aged man grew serious as he pointed to the corner of the cabin where the woodstove was and asked if I had seen it yet. The bottom of the stove had begun to rot out, and the glowing embers inside cast eerie twinkles of light across the ceiling.

"What?" I asked.

"You know, the *cheebuy*," he said.

I knew that "*cheebuy*" meant "ghost" in Ojibwa, and his question startled me at first because I was not immediately sure as to whether he was serious or just testing my knowledge of his language. People were always doing this to me—throwing out words, perhaps giggling a bit, just to see if I knew what they were talking about. I took this as a degree of acceptance.

In this case, the *cheebuy* was apparently that of the deceased Ed Pigeon, the one-armed former owner of my cabin. I had heard about Ed Pigeon before. He was a white man like myself, and the implication apparently was that he might, on account of our similarity of race, reveal himself to me. His skill as a carpenter was widely known, as he once beat out a two-armed man in a strange nail driving contest, adroitly transferring the nails from his mouth to the position on a log in rapid fire succession. He was also a former railway employee and had considerable status on that account. This talk about ghosts and the like made

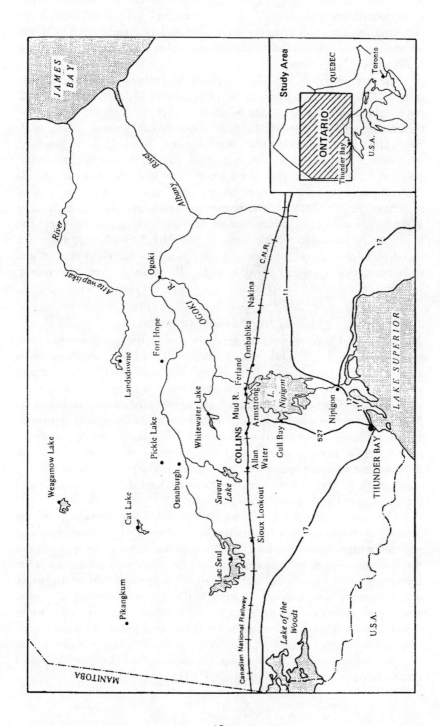

me nervous, because while Ed Pigeon's apparition had not revealed itself to me, I also realized that through the long winter months I had to spend many hours alone in this cabin, and we never know what tricks the mind is apt to play as we work our way through the manifestations, real or imagined, of the so-called "culture shock" experience.

The scene of this cabin and of the people who came and went was real life many years ago; yet it remains with me yet, often in vivid detail. The cabin itself has long been torn down now, the result it is said of the drowning of Sogo, the person from whom I rented the cabin. Without the cabin, the reasoning went, Sogo's ghost would not have a place to settle down and would move elsewhere.

People become apprehensive in unusual or unexplainable circumstances. Sogo's death was one of these. He was a man in his late fifties, had spent all his life in the bush, and was an expert hunter and trapper. He spent the summer months guiding American sport fishers and had built several cabins for them at a lake several miles from the community. One day his boat was seen out in the bay, spinning around in a circle, with no one aboard. Sogo's body was never found, and this made people uneasy. It was just too mysterious to write off as a freak accident—it seemed to some to be the result of some malevolent, supernatural intent.

Organizing our "Realities"

These events had a permanent impact on my psyche; the cumulative nature of such happenings had a subtle moulding effect. They are a touchstone to an alternate reality that is after all these years still only poorly conceived and apprehended on my part. It is as if in the beginning of our fieldwork we are not allowed a true glimpse of the magnitude and scope of the reality enveloping us. In any event we are usually too naive, young and immature to fully appreciate what is going on, so our mind's eye secretly files various occurrences away for safekeeping, as it were, with the possibility that at some later stage of our development we might be in a position to make a more profound sense of these happenings. So these little snippets of time are hauled out on occasion and presented to us for closer scrutiny and analysis.

The trouble with this is that we are now years down the road, and the accuracy of our recollections, even with the aid of written field notes, should be regarded with a degree of scepticism. We appear to have a clear grasp of the detail of some events, but other aspects have been forgotten altogether. What this means is that we are faced with the task of trying to reconstruct the reality of the original fieldwork and all the other "realities" that have emerged over the years, as we reflect on our experiences and what they mean in some wider objective sense. How merry, we are led to think, must be the life of the logical positivist for whom the content of observation tends to be free of conceptual contamination. It is no wonder that Nietzsche called this the "dogma of immaculate perception" (in Kaplan 1964: 131).

Most anthropologists who conduct fieldwork, I suspect, would have little difficulty identifying with the general tenor of this observation about the aftereffects of their research. Yet, most would not spend much time analyzing their recollections, at least not in any systematic manner. It is akin to the way people think about their dreams. Most people probably soon forget about them, but if a particularly disturbing dream haunts them, they may spend some time thinking about the dream as a way of trying to rid themselves of its aftereffects. They may search for an analogy that might provide a key to uncovering some deeper meaning, some undercurrent of concern that is bothering them. Analyzing fieldwork, like analyzing dreams, can help us understand who we are as people and, in a wider sense, the cultural milieu that has spawned us. Ulin notes: "Fieldwork or participant observation has led many anthropologists to struggle with epistemological problems related to understanding other cultures as part of a dialectical process of self-understanding" (1984: xi).

In anthropology, information is gathered mainly on the basis of firsthand experience gained through field research. Therefore, the interrelationship between fieldwork and the creation of knowledge should be a matter of considerable epistemological interest in the discipline, and today it is no longer the case that anthropologists show little interest in the epistemological issues raised by fieldwork. In fact ethnography, especially the way in which the point of view of the "other" is depicted, is at the centre of discussion in contemporary anthropology. One could also argue, with some justification, that anthropologists today are engaged in a debate of considerable importance to the future of the discipline and that debate is largely about fieldwork (or about how anthropologists gather, interpret and synthesize their data) in one form or another. The controversies involved in this debate are multi-faceted ones, but at the centre of it all is a call for a distinct break with the past. The "past" in this case has to do with the more traditional brand of anthropology in which a single (usually) fieldworker conducts a study more a less of his or her own making. The fieldworker decides what to study, the methods used in the investigation and perhaps most importantly, how the results are to be interpreted and disseminated. There is not, in most cases, much of a dialogue between the fieldworker and the informants in the study on matters of methodology, data analysis, publication and so on. In this context, the ethnographer wields considerable authority. The people who are the objects of the study, by contrast, often have considerably less influence on what goes into the study and what emerges on the pages of a book or journal article.

A Crisis of Representation?

In the context of ethnography and fieldwork as a form of power relations involving the dissemination of anthropological knowledge, there is an issue of what has been called a "crisis of representation," which is to say, "the explicit discourse that reflects on the doing and writing of ethnography" (Marcus and

Fisher 1986: 16). The challenge here is to "all those views of reality in social thought which prematurely overlook or reduce cultural diversity for the sake of the capacity to generalize or to affirm universal values" (Marcus and Fisher 1986: 33). From this point of view the chief aim of ethnography ought to concern the worldviews, systems of meanings and values as seen internally, from the native's (emic) vantage point in different cultures.

There is no search in all of this for "scientific truth" or causal points of view. This relativistic stance therefore renders each culture almost totally unique, with no search for how it got that way. We are left then with ethnography consisting of an exercise in cultural interpretation in much the same way that one might "read into" a poem or novel different points of view in the manner of a literary criticism. Furthermore, people like Abu-Lughod (1991) and Keesing (1993) have criticized early anthropology (up to the 1960s) for exaggerating uniqueness and "particularism," of overly emphasizing cultural differences, which translates into "inferiority." It is essentially this viewpoint which is at the heart of current criticisms against the concept of "culture."

Issues such as these are important in contemporary anthropology. This book is not an attempt to engage in a critical discussion of the epistemological implications of the post-modernist tendency in anthropology, but it does fall somewhere in this broad context. In my mind a more interesting and potentially significant task is in the documentation of the ethnographers' role in cultural description.

It is certainly true that the so-called post-modernist approach is much more than literary style, and post-modernism doesn't necessarily mean anti-field-work. It does question anthropological authority and calls for a dialogic approach (which anthropologists have always done anyway to some degree or another). And besides, it is clear that even post-modernist ethnography is controlled by some authority—the fieldworker. All of this would lead me to the view that post-modernism and my "experience" approach are not completely different. After all, my experience approach does hinge in large measure on interpretation (and interpretation is certainly at the heart of Geertz's (1973, 1983) "interpretative" anthropology), and Geertz was one of the main shapers of post-modernism.

What I am saying here is that I distance myself from that strand of post-modernism that (a) reduces fieldwork merely to text and (b) tends to make anthropology into a library (not fieldwork) discipline. However, at the same time, I promote the interpretive aspect of post-modernism, which in my mind is perfectly consonant with my "experience" paradigm. This book, then, can be seen to complement and enrich post-modernism in anthropology by demonstrating how experience shapes eventual interpretation and textual presentation.

I also support the post-modernist argument that the construction of ethnography is largely a matter of organizing our "reflexive understandings" of the fieldwork experience. It is a process fraught with difficulties of interpretation as we attempt to grapple with the accumulation of "realities"—ours and that of the "other"—that have been built up over time. The fact that we are able to provide a plausible account of this experience is an achievement in itself. Our success depends pretty much on how we are able to organize these various understandings. We group them together in various ways, by discussing issues and problems, and thereby build up larger spheres or facets of the account we seek to portray. Thus, this process of constructive understanding becomes central to the problem of verification in fieldwork, given that quite different accounts of the same "reality" can be expected.

Despite our best intentions and preparations, the world has a tendency not to appear as we intend or would like but at times as a *pot pourri* of incongruous situations and events. We strive in various ways to grasp the threads of understanding that make such situations intelligible. We interview, we participate, we observe and we formulate hypothetical constructs. There is a tendency, the more our comprehension and skill are strained, to delve more into the intricacies of methodology. We begin to think that the big barrier is a methodological one and that if only we had a more appropriate or more sophisticated methodological approach, our problems of comprehension would be solved.

The problem for the ethnographer is less a methodological one, that is, in the more narrow sense of various research techniques, than it is with the bigger issue of the sorts of models, paradigms and theoretical orientations that are brought to the interpretation of fieldwork data. However, one is also struck by the apparent tendency for anthropologists to avoid the task of articulating their assumptions and underlying analytical constructs. It is only halfway through a study that certain trends in analysis become evident. We are apt to stop at this point and say, hold it, this person must be a conflict theorist, a cultural materialist or a neo-evolutionist. There is much that is not available for scrutiny in the task of ethnography that makes it difficult to assess where one stands. We all realize that different points of view are possible, even probable, given the diversity of cultural settings in which anthropological research is conducted. Not only must ethnographers deal with the issue of the extent to which their perceptions coincide with those of the people in other cultures, there is the added facet of the researcher's changing viewpoints as material is evaluated, assessed and analyzed.

What is at stake here is an important epistemological question about subjectivity in fieldwork. The issue of the relative importance of the researcher's subjective stance is of course central to the "representation problem," suggesting that the focus of discussion return, as it was once in the past, to this most basic of epistemological concerns for anthropology. A return to a discussion of the inherent dilemmas of fieldwork is therefore called for, founded on the view that the central problems in anthropology are intrinsically tied to fieldwork.

Fieldwork is an ambiguous experience for the anthropologist. Part of the ambiguity stems from the ethnographer's attempt to bridge the gap between objectivity and subjectivity. The general lack of discussion of this problem in relation to field studies has meant that anthropologists have become the subject of criticism on this account, such that "ethnographic accounts are by their very nature one-sided, although based on dyadic interaction" (Manyoni 1983: 227). Whether the reduction or elimination of this "one-sidedness" of fieldwork is possible, or even desirable, is a difficult question to answer.

Much of the turning point for debate in anthropology centres on the issues of how knowledge is created by the researcher in the field. However, when we discuss participant observation, we tend to become apologetic, hoping that no one will seriously challenge what might appear to be an unsophisticated or even an inappropriate method of gathering information. When we talk about unstructured interviewing, we realize in our hearts that it requires considerable skill to conduct and that it is probably our greatest aid in the field; yet we have difficulty in describing what we are doing in a manner that does not appear to be rambling, undisciplined and lacking purpose. Of course, at times our methods do have some of these characteristics, which may not always be such a disadvantage since it leaves open the possibility of serendipitous discovery. We eventually come to learn that the cultivation of methodology is neither sufficient nor necessary for a successful anthropological endeavour, since there is much more that goes into the making of a successful field trip than an armful of specific tools for eliciting information.

In this introductory chapter, I have attempted to summarize several of the key issues in contemporary anthropology as they relate specifically to fieldwork. There are those who would replace the more traditional brand of anthropology, involving hypothesis formation, various methods of data collection and so on, with a heavy emphasis on the interpretive aspects of cultural studies. In this case there is a dissolving of the ethnographer-informant roles and an accent placed on the manner in which cultural phenomena are interpreted and written up. The role of fieldwork in this brand of anthropology is diminished to some degree from what it has been in more recent decades.

The emphasis in this book is on what we have all regarded as implicitly important: experiences in the field. The viewpoint taken is from my own experience conducting research into Aboriginal life in northwestern Ontario, the area I refer to as "Nipigon country." By recounting anecdotes involving the people I met and the situations I became involved in, my hope is to show not only what it was like to conduct anthropology in this area of northern Canada but also how the various seemingly disconnected experiences that happen in the field eventually become interwoven into a larger pattern of social and cultural analysis.

Organization and Style

In writing this book I have two main purposes in mind. One of these is to provide a "documentary" about what it was like for me to conduct fieldwork among the Ojibwa people of northwestern Ontario. My purpose could be seen as an attempt to document a facet of anthropology's history in Canada. I consider it unfortunate that ethnographers have not seen the need to describe what it was like to live in various Canadian places or to tell us what it was like to work with the people who were their subjects. From their more formal publications, we learn about their scholarly and academic interests, but the background information on their fieldwork experiences is lacking. Maybe they felt it not worth writing about, or maybe they felt it was their own business. Whatever the case, aside from the historical interest that such accounts would provide, we would gain scholarly insights, such as the reasons why they studied certain problems or issues relating to documenting and analyzing cultural practices. Perhaps at some later time it might be possible to reconstruct these field experiences from the informal notes that were filed with a museum or granting agency, but these would not be the same as written accounts by the original anthropologists themselves. Take the late Edward Rogers as a case in point. At one time head of the ethnology program of the Royal Ontario Museum, he conducted fieldwork among the Cree and Ojibwa people of Ontario and Quebec from the 1940s into the 1980s. He wrote mainly ethnological and archaeological publications, the main one probably being *The Round Lake Ojibwa* (1962). In the 1970s I was an M.A. student of his at McMaster University, where he taught a course called "Contemporary North American Native People." What I found most interesting in his course were the background anecdotes and off-hand descriptions of the people he lived with, the sorts of things you don't usually read about in formal ethnographic publications. It is for this reason that I think an account of his life in the eastern subarctic would have made fascinating reading and would have been a particularly informative document illustrating the issues and problems of fieldwork in the mid-twentieth century.

While not suggesting that my own career could, or should, be compared with that of Ed Rogers, I do believe any one of us who has conducted fieldwork has a contribution to make to the epistemology of anthropology, to the manner in which knowledge is accumulated and formed. Herein lies the second purpose for writing this book. I want to describe the issues and problems that motivated me to conduct my fieldwork in the first place and how the conditions of this research were modified over time as a result of the problems that emerged during the course of the fieldwork itself.

Fieldwork is not necessarily a straightforward process of investigative reporting. Our problems change as we change. This happens because of the new people we meet, the conditions of their lives and the serendipitous events and occurrences that are a part of fieldwork. Most anthropologists find that the original intention or motivation for conducting the fieldwork becomes altered in significant ways as a result of the process of discovery that is integral to the changing way we see the world over time. As an epistemological issue, it would be useful to know more about the way anthropologists' changing perceptions of research problems is a factor in the final product—the polished ethnography that is finally published.

Throughout most of this work, I write in a "novelistic" or narrative style. I am telling a story about what life was like for me in an Ojibwa village in a remote part of northern Ontario. This book started as a series of stories, some humorous, others tragic, about people and situations. The original field notes were used to "refresh" my memory, but these tales are not strictly a recounting from these notes. Rather, they are reflections or ponderings made years later. Given the large gap in time, I make no pretense to a strict sense of accuracy. On the other hand, to the best of my memory I have not embellished these stories in any way or intentionally included inaccurate details. In any event, it is not so much the accuracy of any of this recounting that is the important issue here. In fact one of the more important points I make about experiences in fieldwork is that there are many subjective points of view possible in describing any situation, any one of which is just about as "accurate" as any other. It is how we interpret these events that I find the most interesting and how our recollections become transformed into the more scholarly or academic treatises that we trick ourselves into thinking are the "original realities" of the fieldwork itself.

In the beginning phase of this writing, I was content with just letting the stories emerge out of my subconscious, one at a time, as a natural process or development. This has led to a *pot pourri* effect that some readers might have difficulty with. I make no apologies here, because as much as we would like "reality" to be coherent, organized, logical and so on, it usually isn't. So my stories, I believe, are a more accurate representation of the reality that I experienced in the field. Things happen as they happen, not as we wish them to happen or in ways that make sense to our research agenda. It is only later that we betray the truth of it all, for the "sake of science," by overlaying our own sense of coherence on the original events and occurrences.

My advice here, then, is to take these vignettes as they are, to try to enjoy them for what they might have to offer in entertainment value, without trying to impute too much scholarly significance or "meaning" to them, although there are also times when I engage in analysis. And the later sections of the book probably have a better flow to them, but I would see this as a reflection of what happens in fieldwork. As time goes on our vision of what is going on becomes more focused, so that we begin to look for certain things to happen, because we are interested in studying these things in their own right to the possible exclusion of others. In the process of this "refinement," we become in slightly greater control of our destinies in the field, in contrast to the floundering that is more characteristic of our early fieldwork.

This does not mean, however, that we are in some kind of reflexive free fall in this book. I have already attempted to enlarge on the discourse of this discussion by tackling certain issues current in anthropology today which I feel are germane to the subject of fieldwork in an epistemological sense. However, I do not want this academic nail biting to intrude too heavily on the fundamental storytelling aspect of the book, so I have restricted discussion of these theoretical/methodological issues to the beginning and concluding sections. In addition, I have tried not to be too heavy handed, or overly academic, in locking horns with this theoretical discourse.

It is my hope that the reader will find the various portraits and episodes somewhat charming in themselves, but I also attempt to place them in a wider context. For this reason, each chapter ends with some observations or reflections. I am in a bit of quandary here: my desire is to introduce a sense of flow and integration, but I suppress this to some extent because it is not necessarily a very accurate depiction of the fieldwork reality. So a bit of a compromise is worked out here, with the work possibly too choppy for some or maybe too smooth for others. Indeed, a major challenge here is to provide a smooth flow to the manuscript, plus deeper reflection and interpretation, without losing the freshness of the "stream of consciousness" approach.

Chapter Two

Research in Nipigon Country

To an ethnographer the shapes of knowledge are always ineluctably local, indivisible from their instruments and encasements. —Clifford Geertz (1983: 4)

Lake Nipigon is one of the largest freshwater lakes in the world. It would be better known perhaps if it were not dwarfed by the largest of them all—Lake Superior. "Nipigon" in Ojibwa (Anishenabe) means "deep, clear water." It is the name given to the lake, the long, meandering river and the small village situated where the Nipigon River empties into Superior. The Trans-Canada Highway linking Sault Ste. Marie with Thunder Bay is one of the few paved roadways in this part of the country. Many people travel by boat or bush plane or along the various dirt roads left over from the pulp cutting days. This is the story of what it is like for me, as an anthropologist, to conduct fieldwork in the northern bush of Nipigon country, the story of my travels and the people I met.

Early Life Experiences

First, I would pose a question about the role of one's early experiences (place of birth, child rearing, educational opportunities and the like) and psychological temperament in an anthropologist's career path. There has been some thought given to this matter over the years, but the relationship between an anthropologist's make-up and the sorts of research he or she does has not been given protracted or serious consideration. Hortense Powdermaker, however, has made some revealing observations on her own life and on some of the social and psychological reasons behind her career choice as an anthropologist:

> Long before I ever heard of anthropology, I was being conditioned for the role of stepping in and out of society. It was part of my growing-up process to question the traditional values and norms of the family and to experiment with behavior patterns and ideologies. This is a not uncommon process of finding one's self.... Why should a contented and satisfied person think of standing outside his or any other society and studying it? (1966: 19–20)

Powdermaker attempts to answer her question by reviewing the life histories of anthropologists. She suggests the emergence of several prominent themes, such as an early concern about social relations and a tendency towards open rebelliousness in the family. From a psychological standpoint, these traits possibly stem from unresolved conflicts over parental relations, leading to a later focus on personal relationships generally. The common theme among scientists generally is that they stand "somewhat apart from life," which Powdermaker suggests is not necessarily an undesirable characteristic because the absorption of scientists in their work could act as a compensatory mechanism for some deep personal needs.

If her suggestion is correct, then we might expect that different trends in anthropology over the years could be correlated in a general way with the changing personality characteristics of those who are attempting to meet their psychological needs. For example, Clyde Kluckhohn has written, "The lure of the strange and far has a peculiar appeal for those who are dissatisfied with themselves or who do not feel at home in their own society" (1957: 11). Similarly, Barrett (1979) describes anthropologists as "marginal academics," choosing to exist outside of the mainstream of conventional intellectual life of the university. Their fieldwork in apparently exotic places stands in sharp contrast to the mundane world of routine laboratory experiments of other scientists. Fieldwork in anthropology is associated with a certain mystique, fuelled by a sense of adventure, epitomized, for example, by the subtitle to Martha Ward's (1989) account of fieldwork: *Adventures in Anthropology on a Tropical Island.*

It is Barrett's contention that some anthropologists intentionally contribute to this aura or sense of mystique and adventure, regaling the guests at departmental parties with their stories of the strange foods, social customs, dress and sexual practices of "primitive" tribes. In the classroom, too, first-year students are introduced to this fascination with the exotic. The suggestion is that it is only the anthropologist who is capable of transcending the inscrutable cultural barriers discussed in the textbooks. Who can forget the dramatic scene in the film *Studying the Yanomama* where Napoleon Chagnon enters one of their villages attired only in a loin cloth, body paint and bright red feathers tied to his upper arms? Students get the point: anthropologists are certainly different, if not even a bit weird.

This feeling of "apartness" and of being somewhat different is something I have been able to relate to from an early age. I was born in the late 1940s in the northern Ontario town of Beardmore, on the eastern shore of Lake Nipigon. The town was the site of several large gold mines, business was booming for a while, and my parents moved there from Fort William (now Thunder Bay) so that my father could work as an accountant for a recently established automobile dealership. Beardmore has always been known for its cold temperatures and fierce winters. In fact my mother claims that it was so cold the day after I was born (June 27th) that the flowers set outside her hospital room door actually froze. The streets of the town were lined in winter with huge snowbanks; my mother took a picture of one outside our house which she measured at eighteen feet. In the summer, you could hardly ever sit outdoors because of the intense swarms of mosquitoes.

My mother had grown up in the tranquil, pleasant setting of a southern Ontario farm, and I sensed from an early age her longing for this warm nurturing life and, by contrast, her disdain for Beardmore's harsh social and physical environment. The people of the town, mostly post-war European immigrants, she saw as crude and unsophisticated. Sights such as men spitting their tobacco juice onto the street, drunken brawls and women swearing in public were probably responsible for her sense of distance from the townsfolk.

Our living conditions were quite humble at this time. We started out in a two-room log cabin and then moved into a more modern frame building several months later. I remember my mother's excitement at having a small hand pump right beside the kitchen sink, which meant that she didn't have to carry water from the well anymore. In the winter evenings, after supper, my father usually went out to the back yard and chopped wood for several hours. I remember these as happy times; he laughed and joked, whistling "home on the range" as he hauled logs from the wood pile. Usually he would stack several pieces of wood onto my outstretched arms for me to carry back into the house. I couldn't have been prouder than when I presented these to my mother to place beside the cook stove. Looking back now, I see that our neighbours were a peculiar lot, although I didn't think so at the time. Out in their front yard was a tall pole, with a small platform on top. Chained to this pole was their pet, a bear cub, who would scamper up and stay perched on its roost for most of the day.

My mother had a sense of empathy with the Ojibwa people of Beardmore, though, possibly identifying with their marginality. For example, she claims to have given Norval Morriseau, who later became a famous Aboriginal painter, art supplies when he was a teenager living with his grandfather. My mother was also forever grateful to a young Ojibwa woman, Josephine Nakanajos, who saved me from drowning when I was three years old. As the story goes, I was following several children as they walked across a small, ice covered pond. Josephine noticed that I hadn't returned from the pond area and went down to investigate. She discovered that I had fallen through the ice and was floating face down, buoyed up only by my homemade snowsuit. After fishing me out, she carried me back home, where my horrified mother rocked me over her knees, pushing the water out of my lungs. The story of this rescue was subsequently written up in a Thunder Bay newspaper. Whether this event had anything to do with it or not, in our household, I never heard Native people discussed in disparaging terms, but only of their intelligent adaptation to a harsh bush environment, their artistic qualities, and the spirituality and dignity of their culture.

By the early 1950s, we moved farther down the highway to Nipigon, a town of about two thousand people on the north shore of Lake Superior. It didn't take long for my father to establish his own car dealership, and his business prospered in the post-war economy. My life was spent pumping gas at my Dad's garage, delivering newspapers, playing hockey and baseball, practising my slingshot, riding my bike, fishing and hunting for partridge after school with my .22 rifle. I remember spending much of my time by myself. As I delivered papers, I would stop to build a small house in the bush and daydream about life in the outdoors. As a young teenager I once contemplated taking my rifle, fishing rod and hatchet and trying to make a living off the land for some extended period of time. I did have some skills in this area, as I spent much of my younger life in Boy Scouts, proudly attaining badges for outdoor pursuits. On several occasions our troop went camping in the winter. We slept on a thick layer of pine boughs inside a carefully crafted lean-to set up against a face of rock. A fire was made to burn up next to this rock facing, that in turn radiated heat throughout the night. Perhaps I saw myself living off the land the way First Nations people had in previous times, but in hindsight it probably would have been foolish to attempt such a feat.

Any sense of achievement that I might have received from the outdoor life, however, was not reflected in my school life. Generally I was bored with the whole affair and had to repeat my final year of high school. More than anything, I wanted to get on with life and be an "adult," as I understood the term. This led to marriage at age nineteen and moving to work at the Inco nickel mine in Thompson, Manitoba, in 1967, Canada's centennial year.

Life was hard in Thompson. My idyllic sense of "being an adult" was tempered by long overtime shifts; often I worked seven days a week. I also took a truck driving job on the mine site for a private contractor, so there were times when several days would go by before I would leave the site. The climate was also very harsh. I remember three feet of snow falling just after the Labour Day weekend in September and it not melting until June. It was so cold in January that the tires on a car had a permanent flat spot on them from sitting in the frigid sixty below temperature overnight. They made a weird "thump-thump" sound as the car went down the street. One January evening, after I had worked a double shift, my car wouldn't start, so I hitched a ride downtown and then almost froze to death walking home to my apartment on the outskirts of town. I particularly remember how the pain of the cold, driving wind suddenly turned to a warm, balmy breeze and I was filled with thoughts of resting for a while on the snow bank. All the way home I fought the overpowering urge to have a little "death sleep" on the side of the road.

The one thing that life in Thompson taught me was that if I worked hard I could make a lot of money. But I also learned that life in the mine, despite the money, didn't have any long-term appeal for me. I had a vision of making something of myself, of having a career doing something I enjoyed. A new start was in order, and this meant enrolling at Lakehead University in Thunder Bay. My high school marks were so low that I had to enroll as an adult student, which I was able to do since I had just turned twenty-one.

My recollection of university life was that I felt years older than the other students. They wanted to party, but I wanted to work hard at my school work.

The luxury of reading in the library, planning an essay or sitting in lectures was in such contrast to my previous life as a miner that I appreciated having the time to do something for myself. As a new student I wasn't sure what courses to take. After enrolling in the mandatory courses of English, French and history, I was intrigued with the subject of anthropology. I associated anthropology with ancient society, like the Egypt of the books my mother had at home. My idea was to become a history major, and one of the counsellors in the history department said that he didn't really know what anthropology was so he would take me to meet an anthropologist. He knocked on one office door after another and could find no one. I concluded from this that anthropologists were the smart ones. They were off doing interesting things while the historians were doing counselling duties with undergraduate students.

I liked my introductory course in anthropology so much that I decided to drop all my history courses and replace them with anthropology. I remember my father warning me against such a move—"How will you ever find any work when you are finished?" There was one thing I knew about myself, though, and that was that if I lacked a burning desire in a subject, then it wouldn't sustain me in the years ahead. Anthropology provided that fervent interest. What appealed to me most was the very broad scope of the discipline—you could explore all time periods, biological and evolutionary trends or linguistic diversity, in a multitude of cultural settings.

In my first year, most of my grades were in the "C" and "D" category. Partly this was due to deficiencies in my high-school background, but the low marks were also a result of my poor performance on exams, especially multiple choice questions. By my second year, though, there was much more emphasis placed on writing essays and exercising one's individual initiative. In this environment I performed much better, as I found that I had a knack for writing and loved the challenge of working alone on projects. My grades soared upwards, along with my enthusiasm for anthropology.

I like to relate my story to students who feel discouraged with the way things are going with their studies. I tell them to try to find things that interest them, because when we are interested in something, our motivation to learn increases. I tell them about my working life in the mine at Thompson and how I appreciated the opportunity to read and write without being controlled by a time clock. I tell them about my poor marks at the beginning but how I persevered and achieved good results in the end. The lesson I want to relate is that it is important in life to look inside ourselves for the inner strengths that we all possess and to try to make use of our own skills and interests so that learning becomes an enjoyable experience.

One of the experiences that made an immense difference for me was meeting an anthropologist by the name of P.J. "Jud" Epling in my final year at Lakehead. Jud had recently left the Riverside campus at the University of California in Los Angeles and had come to Thunder Bay on a one-year replacement exchange with Theodore "Teddy" Kreps, who in turn, went to

California. Jud took me on as an informal research assistant. We worked on his publications, and he would give me course credits. At the time he was engaged in a project concerning a quantitative analysis of Polynesian sibling terminologies, which was eventually published in *American Anthropologist*. He also had conducted fieldwork in Australia, with Joe Birdsell while an M.A. student at the University of Chicago, and later in Samoa.

Jud amazed me. He seemed to know all the big names in American anthropology and was friends with many of them. Jud also knew how to write articles and get them published in the top journals. It was Jud who encouraged me to go to graduate school and who wrote letters of recommendation on my behalf. Eventually I chose to go to McMaster, in Hamilton, because the people there, such as Ruth Landes, Richard Slobodin and Ed Rogers, were experts on subarctic Aboriginal ethnology. Jud subsequently moved on to the Department of Epidemiology, at Chapel Hill, North Carolina. I have never forgotten the encouragement he gave me and sense of enthusiasm for anthropology that he shared with me.

Another turning point occurred in 1972, when the American Anthropological Association annual meeting was held at the Royal York Hotel in Toronto. As a new grad student at McMaster, I shared with my schoolmates a rush of excitement at attending these meetings. All the big names were there. At one point I was bold enough to crash a party in one of the hotel rooms. Bursting in, I was handed a drink and before long found myself sitting on the floor chatting with Marvin Harris. I also had a long chat with Jud's own mentor, Kim Romney, from California. It was as if I was undergoing a crash course in "anthropological enculturation." For one of the first times in my life, I felt part of something, apparently accepted by some of the most revered people in the discipline.

There is one final anecdote that I want to relate about these AAA meetings. It happened just after I decided to return home, in the early evening, as I was tired from attending a number of sessions. Walking down a long corridor in the hotel, I noticed a person silhouetted against an end window. The caped figure carried what looked like a long staff. Then it hit me; this was Margaret Mead coming towards me. My first instinct was to make a retreat in the other direction. However an inner voice told me that this was an opportunity for me that I would later regret not taking. So, exercising as much pluck as possible, I approached her.

"Excuse me, Dr. Mead," I said. "I am a student of your friend Ruth Landes at McMaster, and I wonder if I could walk with you for a minute?"

"Here, let me get a hold of your arm, young man," she replied, as she slipped her arm in mine, "and how is Ruth these days?" She talked a little about their days together as students with Frans Boas, but I don't remember too much else about the conversation. Finally, she stopped and indicated the room that she was going to. Suddenly, two large double doors swung open, and a crowd of perhaps five or six hundred people rose to their feet, clapping their hands as they did so. Margaret Mead seemed to float upwards onto the elevated stage, as if her cape were a set of wings. I was dumbfounded by this unexpected experience, this encounter with one of the icons of anthropology. I couldn't bring myself to follow her into the room, so I turned and left and continued home to Hamilton.

At McMaster, I completed a masters' thesis on kinship systems and information theory, continuing research that Jud and I had begun earlier at Lakehead. In later years, I was to publish a number of articles on the basis of this work—focusing on the historical reconstruction of kinship terminology, Athapaskan and Algonkian sibling terminologies and the role of information theory in kinship relations. I also took the course with Ed Rogers (mentioned previously), whose classes planted seeds of inspiration that I was to later follow.

It was some time during this year at McMaster that I decided to push forward by studying for a doctorate, possibly based on some original research of my own in northwestern Ontario. I felt comfortable with the idea of living in the woods north of Lake Superior, in the area where I grew up. I had made some good contacts along the way as well. While I was in my final year at Lakehead, my younger brother had landed a teaching job in an Ojibwa community called Collins, situated along the Canadian National Railway (CNR) line west of Lake Nipigon. He invited me to come up for a visit, which I originally planned would last for a day or two, but which stretched to include most of the summer. I started to know the people in Collins, and a plan began to form in my mind that if I ever had the opportunity to further my graduate studies, then this small community on the rail-line would be an ideal place to begin such a project. The opportunity for such fieldwork came two years later when I was fortunate enough to be accepted into the Ph.D. program at McGill University in Montreal.

The Research Project at Collins

Now I was situated among the grad students at McGill. We spent many hours sitting around talking about our fieldwork proposals, about their theoretical importance and about where in the world we would like to go. Some were going to the Middle East, another to New Guinea, another to Brazil and others to various exotic places. My own sense in all of this was that as Canadians we should not ignore our own country. Some anthropologists, I suggested, should spend time studying the cultures in Canada, although I had at the time only a distant, and perhaps romanticized, comprehension of the tribulations in-volved—the mosquitoes, loneliness, blowing snow. But I was to discover the many rewarding aspects as well, especially the warmth, goodwill and optimism of the people I would come to live with.

My academic interest was in the Ojibwa people who lived in the small villages scattered along the CNR line from Armstrong to Sioux Lookout. Initially, my ethnographic goals for conducting fieldwork in this area of the north involved several considerations. My first interest started with the realization that there were many First Nations communities in northwestern

Ontario that were not official "Indian reserves," according to the legal definition set out in Canada's *Indian Act*. Some people referred to them as "squatter" communities, but I preferred to call them "non-reserve Indian communities." Many such places are comprised of Native people who have lost their right to live on a reserve because their Indian status had been taken away from them, mainly as a result of Indian women marrying men (white or otherwise) who did not have status. Such communities of "non-status" Native people have sprung up outside the official reserves and are fairly common in Canada's north country. In addition, many Native people moved off their reserves because of the economic hardships, such as a lack of adequate housing and employment on the reserve. Unfortunately, these non-reserve communities often provided fewer benefits than existed on reserves and the plight of these people might well have worsened as a result of their off-reserve migration. These communities might have a combination of status, non-status, Metis and Euro-Canadian people living in them.

As I scoured the ethnographic literature on Canadian First Nations, I found that virtually all of the research dealt only with "Indian" reserves—there was hardly any mention at all of the "non-reserve" side of life. It was almost as if one had to live on a reserve to be considered a Native person in Canada. I began to develop a research proposal around this notion of investigating the non-reserve aspects of First Nations life in Canada. I wondered, for example, about the social organization of such communities—were they similar to or different than their reserve counterparts? What was their history; how were they formed? How about their leadership structure? On reserves, leaders are usually elected to their positions—do non-reserve communities continue with this style of leadership or do they develop their own patterns? What about their relationships with outside government agencies? On reserves, the federal Department of Indian and Northern Affairs (DIAND) has almost complete jurisdictional and administrative control. Does this apply to non-reserves? Does the provincial government take over in some manner? Or are they treated the same as non-Native communities? The argument that I wanted to put forward as a rationale for my anthropological research was that an ethnographic literature that only represented reserve Native communities was one-sided and incomplete. In sum, I thought that an original contribution could be made to the anthropology of Canadian communities by studying the social, economic and political organization of those Native communities existing outside of DIAND's administrative structure.

I had my start on a research proposal, but I wanted to push it further, beyond a mere ethnographic contribution into more theoretical grounds. I reasoned that if I could use this research on non-reserve communities in a wider context, then its appeal to other anthropologists would be more far reaching than if I restricted the research to narrow objectives.

When I began to explore the anthropological research on politics and leadership patterns, what stood out was a considerable body of literature on what was called "patron-client relationships." Most of these studies described how community leaders (the patrons) dispense favours of various sorts (jobs, help with legal problems, housing and so on) to their followers (or clients). This type of leadership pattern was described in several parts of the world, but the literature was particularly focused on central and south America and the Mediterranean region. The patron-client style of leadership is often a characteristic of small communities that lack more formal institutional structures or regularized ties with outside government agencies. Local people who have a variety of different skills, such as some knowledge of the legal system, who are literate or who have contacts in government circles, for example, step into informal leadership positions, attracting about them people who lack these skills or contacts themselves.

It became evident to me that these non-reserve First Nations communities had many of the same characteristics, particularly the lack of formal leadership structures and well-defined links and access to government service-providing agencies, as the small towns and villages described in the anthropological literature. I wondered if the non-reserve community would therefore also tend to depend on so-called "patrons" to provide leadership needs. There were definite parallels between the type of First Nations community that I wanted to study and the type described in the anthropology literature, but I needed to open up more avenues of investigation. This began to develop when I read more of the literature in political anthropology and saw that the descriptions of patron-client relations tended to ignore the cultural and social environments in which they occurred. This was the opening I was looking for—one that would allow me to link my more specific ethnographic interest in northern First Nations communities with the wider theoretical literature in anthropology as a whole.

As my focus became more refined, I put forward the proposition that one could expect different types of patron-client relationships to emerge in different cultural and social contexts, in contrast to examples in the literature which tended to convey the impression of more uniform political relationships despite differences in cultural background. For example, traditional First Nations leadership placed a strong emphasis on generosity and non-interference in the personal affairs of others. Would these factors, I questioned, make the sorts of patron-client relations that occur in non-reserve communities different from those found in other areas of the world? And what about the economic advantages, in terms of the favours, privileges and goods that leaders dispense to followers? Given the hunting societies of northern Canada and the modest accumulation of material goods—would these characteristics condition leadership along particular social and environmental lines?

I felt that with all these questions I was beginning to develop a solid ethnographic and theoretical focus. Not only did I have a number of important questions that I would seek answers to, I was also beginning to develop the sort of research agenda that would guide my fieldwork into providing material that could be used to make some real contributions to northern First Nations ethnography on the one hand and the wider spheres of political and economic anthropology on the other.

Travel in Nipigon Country

My destination was the village of Collins, named after a surveyor for the CNR. It is possible to drive between Armstrong and Thunder Bay, a distance of about 250 km., but the road can be treacherous, as I found out on one of my first trips. I had borrowed my brother's beat-up Chevy Nova and had left it at the Armstrong train station while I was living in Collins, some thirty miles west. The train arrived from Collins around midnight. There was the usual flurry of people around the Armstrong station, but the April weather was still cold enough to prevent any lingering. It was a clear, moonlit night, and I decided to take my chances by driving down to Thunder Bay. I left with the knowledge that there would be no one else on the road at this time of night and no help should I get into some kind of difficulty. What could happen anyway, I thought?

As it turned out, the road was mostly made up of frozen mud, with deep grooves carved into it by car and truck tires during the warmer period of the day. The first several hours went along as well as could be expected, at a much slower pace than one would want, but progress was still being made. Then, just near the reserve of Gull Bay, I was suddenly faced with a vast expanse of water. Apparently, a creek or small river, backed up by the ice, had flooded the road. I didn't want to turn back to Armstrong, and the prospect of sitting there all night waiting for help to come along was something that didn't appeal to me either. So I decided to back the car up, make a run into the water and take my chances.

The car ploughed in about twenty yards and then promptly stalled. Now I was really stuck. My feet felt wet, and I looked down to see the water flowing under the passenger door, over the transmission hump and out the other side. There wasn't much to do except to take a look under the hood, but there was no way that I was going to put my feet into that icy water. I pulled an old T-shirt out of my pack in the back seat, eased the door open, and proceeded to crawl along the fender. Perched like a little monkey on the bumper, I opened the hood and found that at least the motor was not immersed in water—the stream flowed under the oil pan. I began to dry the spark plug wires, coil, distributor and other various ignition parts with the shirt. Slinking back along the fender and into the front seat, I was quite surprised when the car started on the first try. The secret to this whole act of survival was to creep along, so as not to churn up too much water. I had to perform this operation several more times, but eventually managed to traverse this river bed.

I shouldn't have congratulated myself too quickly though, because before I knew it the car got hung up on the frozen ruts. I tried spinning the wheels, but nothing happened, as the rear axle was suspended in mid-air. There's a trick to getting out of a situation like this, but it involves a lot of work. First you have to jack the car up in the middle of the back bumper as far as it will go, so it will sort of swing back and forth. You then push the car off the jack, making sure to side step the pieces of the jack that invariably come shooting out at you. The same operation is then performed at the front of the car, then at the back again, and so forth. Each time you are able to gain several feet, until the car finally rests on the shoulder of the road, away from the ruts in the middle. This procedure got me free of the treacherous groves, allowing me to travel, after many hours of hard work in the middle of the night, on my merry way.

Of course my life in Nipigon country was not always this difficult, but the tale does give an idea of the sort of problems that one could expect to have to deal with at almost any time. Life is full of various challenges, some big and some little. As an anthropologist you may have to draw on your own resources, usually in situations that you would never expect to find yourself, in order to get on with the larger task of collecting information for the field study.

Getting Started

The residents of Collins call their village "Hollywood" because they envision it as a sort of soap opera place filled with adventure, love affairs and tragic twists of fate. As an anthropologist, I saw it as a quaint little place—small log cabins, wood smoke in the air, bear skins stretched out to dry and blueberries everywhere in the late summer. It's the sort of pioneer village that would have been common in southern Ontario a hundred years ago or more. To the outsider it might seem a living anachronism, but the people who live there do not see it that way. For them it makes perfect sense to make a living with the resources that the forest provides—the logs for house construction and heating, and fish and animals for food.

The community of Collins is situated on the CNR line, which passes through northwestern Ontario over the top of Lake Nipigon. The CNR was completed in 1911, and soon after, a series of trading posts and stores were established at various stops along the line. These "line stores" were fairly successful economic operations because their transportation costs were less than those of the more remote, northerly Hudson's Bay Company posts along the Albany River. By the 1940s, increasingly large numbers of Native trappers from such places as Fort Hope and Ogoki would bring their furs down to trade at rail-line stores. Many of the trappers also brought their families and set up their tents around the stores for the summer months. These were occasions for the people to socialize, conduct ceremonies and renew acquaintances. During the 1950s, priests from the Anglican and Roman Catholic faiths began to offer religious and educational instruction to the children before their parents returned to the traplines up north.

Churches were later constructed at a number of these rail-line locations which, along with the store and railway crews, provided a nexus for the incipient settlements. Schools were eventually built, in the early 1960s, and many families constructed log cabins around the churches and stores, moving back and forth between these cabins and their traplines. Collins became a major focus for this demographic shift in population movement and settlement. The village came to be populated mainly by Ojibwa people from the Fort Hope area, but other families from the White Sand and Nipigon House bands around Lake Nipigon to the east also took up residence in Collins.

As the village grew and developed, the major portion of the population became compressed between the rail line and the northern portion of Collins Lake. At the centre of the village is a large clearing comprising the trading store and school, tall jack pines, a series of wide foot paths, and log cabins scattered along the lakeshore. Houses in the village are interconnected by a maze of sandy paths and are clustered together in neighbourhoods according to kinship and band affiliation ties. Except for the teacher's house, a storekeeper's residence, and several CNR houses, all of the approximately thirty houses in the village are constructed of horizontal logs and heated by woodstoves.

During the time of my fieldwork, the Collins population was at about 150, but not all of these people were in the village at any given time since some were outside the area on a temporary basis attending school or working. About sixty percent of the Aboriginal people had retained their Indian status since moving from their home-reserve communities, but many had lost it as a result of their marriage, or their parent's, to a non-status individual. There was a considerable variation in household composition, ranging from households with only one individual to those with as many as four adult members resident at the same time. The most common household type was that of the nuclear family, that is, a couple with dependent children. There were also a considerable number of extended families consisting of nuclear units with other relatives.

The Canadian National Railway, employing a section crew of five men, was the only source of full-time employment for the community. The railway also hired additional men during the summer months for track repairs and other projects. The Ogoki River Guides (ORG), a local village corporation, had initiated several work projects, the largest of which was the construction of a tourist lodge at Whitewater Lake, 80 km north of Collins. All of its projects were sponsored by various federal and provincial agencies. Collins people also earned income through such seasonal employment as trapping, guiding for tourists and the sale of handicrafts.

Day-to-Day Life

My own quarters consisted of a cabin, barely twelve-foot square, that seemed to be in constant need of repair. I was kept busy putting tar on the roof, making a window from a sheet of plastic, painting the floor, building makeshift cupboards or trying to sort out the internal workings of a borrowed oil stove. Eventually the cabin became liveable enough, and its small dimensions made it easy to heat in winter. The cabin was also an important contributing factor to my own sense of belonging in the village. It gave me a sense of identity, a specific location to call my own and a private place to meet my new friends.

It wasn't long before I settled into a daily routine of activities. Usually I got dressed about 8 a.m., grabbed my water buckets and headed out to the water pump across the tracks. There were always a few people, mostly women, lingering there. They talked about the usual sorts of things—the weather, their families, any gossip about the night or day before. The conversation was usually in Ojibwa, so mostly I just listened as best as I could, nodding a few "*bojoo's*," as I waited my place in line. The water sloshed back and forth in the pails, usually soaking my shoes and pant legs, as I plodded along across the open field in front of Peter's store and then through the narrow path up to my cabin.

I poured the fresh water into two saucepans and placed them on the burners of my small, countertop propane stove. The water began to boil quickly and I poured some of it into a plastic washbasin. On cold mornings I found it comforting to breathe in the warm vapours billowing up to my face. Most of the time I quickly brushed my teeth, washed and shaved and then flung the gray water out the front door. The water in the other pan was the used to make oatmeal, something I found would stick in my stomach so I wouldn't feel hungry for a few hours.

After straightening up the dishes, I moved over to the small desk in the other corner of the cabin. From here I could peer out the window, watch people come and go to the store or glance down to the dock area by the lakeshore. There were a few routines that I followed. One was to take out my old Ojibwa dictionary and grammar (published by Rev. Edward Wilson in 1874). I was amazed at how many words and sentence structures had stayed the same over the last century or so. I opened the book at a vocabulary list I had been working on the day before, usually selecting about ten or so words to work on for that day. I wrote them out several times on a sheet of paper and reminded myself to listen for these particular words in the conversations that I would overhear during the day. Sometimes a young fellow called Steve, an acquaintance from our tree planting days five years earlier, came over to visit about this time, and we would go over pronunciation and conversational idioms. This work with Steve was of immense help to me—I could learn words from the book, but I needed someone to clue me in on how to use them in everyday conversation. Often, I said things in a stilted or too formal way that the people found peculiar or funny. Steve corrected me, explaining what the problem was and filling me in on more appropriate forms of expression.

After these linguistic lessons, I often pulled out my field notes, which for me were more a set of daily diaries. I tried to get a sense of how the daily round of activities in the village might be fitting into some larger, over-all pattern. What did I need to work on today? Were there theoretical issues that needed to be substantiated by the collection of some specific details or facts? Who were the people that could help me in particular areas? I tried to get a vision about where I was in my fieldwork and what I had to do that day in order to provide some continuity for the project as a whole.

A useful way of organizing my material was to store it in several notebooks. One, for example, was for economic details—incomes, expenditures, transfer payments—everything I could learn about the economic lives of the people. I was particularly interested in developing contrasts among the economic situations of families along a range of income levels. Families whose men worked on the railway, for example, had relatively high incomes. How did they spend their money? Did they have a purpose or design for their purchases? Did they spend much at the store for food? How about the poorer families, those dependent on seasonal work, welfare or old age pensions? How were their expenditure patterns different from those more well off in money terms?

I kept trying to develop a focus or rationale for the economic statistics and figures I was collecting, at times visualizing how these would be organized in tables and charts or how a particular chapter would be put together, pushing one academic argument or another, substantiated by the various facts I had gathered. By going through this "mock argument" process, I could get a better picture of where my project was going or could go and the holes that I needed to fill if I were to mount a defence of one particular theoretical point of view or another.

In a similar manner, I kept a notebook on the social organizational aspects of the community, developing profiles, for example, on household compositions, kinship ties among individuals and households, the neighbourhood clustering of houses and families or age groups and population pyramids. Here again, I searched for new ways of looking at my social data, realizing that once I had left Collins I wouldn't have much of an opportunity to come back and collect this material again. Any missed data could turn out to be crucial to an argument that I would possibly make at some later date, back at the university in Montreal. I had to keep reminding myself to be as thorough as possible in collecting the basic material while I was still there in the field. I reasoned that the strength of anything I would later write would be pretty much dependent on how well the field material had originally been collected. I could argue a case one way or another, at some later point in time, but I could never make up for deficiencies in my original fieldwork.

After these early morning routines were finished, it was usually about ten or eleven o'clock, at which time it was my practice to head over to Peter's house. A late riser, he was often shaving and getting cleaned up as I arrived, and he would settle down with a cup of coffee. His brother Donald was usually there as well, probably having arrived an hour or two before. Sometimes there was some joking about which fellow was "fooling around" (they called it "gigging") with which women, but it did not take us very long to get down to the important business matters of the day. This usually involved how the negotiations were going with various government agencies over the funding of their tourist lodge project. When the mail came in, we searched through it for correspondence from the personnel in these agencies, which we then discussed in light of whatever strategy we were working on at the time.

I use the word "we" because I felt part of a group effort. There was a mutual aid or reinforcing aspect to my relationship with Peter and Donald. I acted as a sympathetic third party, a "sounding board" if you like, that they could run their ideas by. After listening to their plans or proposals, I provided a mini analysis or commentary, at times suggesting ways they might strengthen their case. On several occasions, I wrote letters for them to government agencies, using their ideas but my more academic vocabulary and writing skill. For my part, I learned quite a bit about being a participant in Collins' political planning and economic development enterprises. Peter, for example, showed me his desk and told me to feel free to pore over the various letters and other correspondence. I filled other notebooks, copying out letters or pulling out phrases that I might later use in quotes. This was all of immense help to me in comprehending the "other side" or governmental point of view with regards the Collins enterprises. I began to see a larger picture about how the local versus outside views over development issues merged, or were different, at various points in time.

By now it was about time for lunch. Dorothy, Peter's wife, would come in from the kitchen with more coffee and a tray with various leftovers from yesterday's supper. Roast beaver meat was one of my favourites, but we also ate, on occasion, geese, duck, fish, moose meat, or whatever else was available at that time of year. Much of this "country food" came from Dorothy's sister, whose husband did a lot of hunting and fishing, despite his job as section foreman for the CNR. Peter and Donald, on the other hand, did very little of these activities.

After filling up on delicious food, it was my habit to wander around the village by myself, talking with whomever I happened to run into. Usually the men were working outside Collins during the day; the women I encountered usually just put their heads down and scurried by. There are numerous trails leading out of the village that I explored during my leisure time—some led down to the lake and along the shoreline; others led north of the village across the railway tracks and out to nearby lakes or the graveyard.

The graveyard, I found, was a most unusual place. Many of the graves had small houses, or roofs, built over them, as if the dear departed continued to need some sort of shelter. I spent a lot of time there, documenting the names of the deceased, when they lived and any other comments that might be recorded on the grave markers. I had never heard of some of the names, and when the appropriate opportunity arose, I asked relatives about them and what had happened. Of course, this was a sensitive subject for most, and I didn't care to have to do it, but felt I should for the sake of the project.

By mid-afternoon, I headed back to my cabin, mostly to do a little reading, think about what I had learned so far that day, have a little nap or whatever. My supper hour was spent either back over at Peter's, if I was invited, which was quite frequently, or at my own place. For supper, I most often boiled up some spaghetti, then poured some sauce over it. I could only keep food on hand that wouldn't spoil, such as pasta or other dried foods. Canned goods were not very convenient because of their weight and the need to carry them from the stores in Armstrong or Savant Lake. Peter's store actually was not very well stocked. On occasion, a large order would come in from Winnipeg, but it would be sold out quickly. During the winter months, food was obviously easier to store; I even made a sort of fridge outside my cabin by digging into the snow which was packed up against the outside wall. I placed perishable food into this cache and covered it up with a large piece of plywood. Surprisingly, I never caught any dogs digging around there, something I expected might happen.

After supper, I frequently found myself back over at Peter's house. In the evening, there was usually a fairly large social gathering there. Among the assembled crowd might be the school teacher, Dorothy's parents and sister, her husband Mike, or any number of other people, such as Rev. Long, the Anglican minister, government people who were staying overnight, bush pilots and a steady stream of village people who dropped by the back entrance to Peter's house to pick up their mail or just chat briefly. By about ten-thirty, everyone had left except Peter and me. We had a lot of heart-to-heart talks during these times, and thinking about these times now, I realize how very much I miss those quiet, reflective conversations on the state of Collins or the world at large. I enjoyed Peter's wit, his insight into human nature and his genuine sympathy for the plight of his community. Peter had his feet in two worlds—because of his roots in his father's Scottish fur trade tradition, he knew the side of business and Europeans; on the other hand, the fact that his mother was Ojibwa allowed him to know things that white Canadians couldn't possibly know of Aboriginal culture and worldview. Peter and I often walked outside in the evening, looking at the stars and sharing our dreams.

I closed my day by returning to my cabin and lighting up the coal oil lamp on my desk. I relaxed by listening to the many American stations I could get on my radio and by playing solitaire. Around eleven or eleven thirty, I blew out the lamp, crawled into the luxurious warmth of my Wood's "five star" eiderdown sleeping bag and quickly drifted off to sleep.

Fieldwork Difficulties

At the beginning of my fieldwork experiences in Collins, I envisioned my task as some kind of heroic endeavour. It may sound a bit trite now, but here I was enduring all these hardships of life in the northern bush for the sake of pushing back the frontiers of knowledge. I was sustained for quite some time by the novelty of the fieldwork experience and the rush of enthusiasm that comes from discovering new facts and ideas. My effort was sustained, too, by a sense of communion with the other northern ethnographers—Skinner, Landes, Hallowell, Dunning and Rogers—that had gone before me. There was a kinship here, linking me with my anthropological clan members. I was carrying on a tradition of scholarship, enduring what others before me had also endured, lending some credence to my fledgling efforts.

Of course it didn't take a lot of time for the reality of where I was and what I was doing to sink in. The lustre wore off of this epic quest, and it was reduced at times to a matter of everyday survival. There were mornings when I didn't want to get out of my sleeping bag, days when I felt a genuine dislike for this isolated little village and the people in it. It came as a shock to realize that most people probably didn't care all that much for me or had little or no interest in my valorous quest for knowledge.

Little things about the people began to bother me. At times it was their malicious sense of humour. One time five or six people were standing around Peter's living room, probably to pick up their mail, when the school teacher's stout ten-year-old daughter walked in. A large, heavy-set man made a reference in Ojibwa to a *kookoosh*, meaning "pig," which brought about loud laughter from the crowd. I found it odd at the time that, since the girl was Native herself, the people were not more sympathetic towards her. Her mother, the teacher, was from the Six Nations reserve in southern Ontario but was usually treated like a white person. Since she did not know the Ojibwa language nor much about their culture, she was probably thought of as just another outsider. She was no doubt disappointed that she was not more readily accepted because I'm sure she saw herself in a general sense as "one of them" and had made a personal sacrifice to come all this way up north to teach in a school that had considerable difficulty attracting teachers.

This matter of acceptance was possibly also at the root of some of my own difficulties. I did make some effort at "fitting in." I ate the local food rather than import large stocks of food from outside, which was what the teachers usually did. My cabin was not significantly different from typical housing in the village. After several months I was able to follow conversations in Ojibwa, not perfectly, but well enough to get the drift of what was being said. When appropriate, I attempted to respond to questions using the local language, which was something that outsiders rarely did.

In the beginning, I had a steady stream of visitors arriving at my door. Most of the time they just peeked in and uttered something to the effect of, "Is Sogo here?" Sogo was the owner of the cabin, and he used to stay there when he visited town, before I moved in. Most of the time I suspected that the people's desire to visit Sogo was really just a ploy to find out what I was up to, but I really didn't mind because I wanted to meet people and to have them feel comfortable about coming around.

As time went on, the visits became less frequent, which I took to indicate that the people were just not that curious about me any more and that maybe they even had come to accept my presence in their village to some extent. Although their visiting at times conflicted with my own personal life, I wanted to "keep the door open" as much as possible, because, ultimately, I was only in the village to conduct research and gather information, and I needed the cooperation of the people in order to carry out this task. Nonetheless, this created a conflict with my sense of personal privacy.

On occasion, I felt used by people's visits, such as the time the CNR foreman came to my place late at night because his wife had kicked him out when he came home drunk. He was obviously looked for a place "to crash" and he literally did just that, falling face first in the middle of the floor. In a matter of seconds he was curled up and snoring, so I just left him in that position, went to bed and in the early morning he was gone. Sometimes people arrived looking for some sort of medical attention, as they were under the mistaken impression that I was some kind of doctor or at least one in training. On the positive side of this sort of visiting, people did feel free to come to me about their personal difficulties, although they were often under the influence at these times, perhaps as a way of buoying up their courage. I began to realize that people might regard an anthropologist is a good person to talk to because they are usually not judgemental, are sympathetic listeners and their position as an outsider means they are less likely to spread the information around the village.

Apathy and boredom were two of my greatest difficulties. There were periods when I just wanted to isolate myself from the village life around me. The research project became too much of a twenty-four-hour-a-day monkey on my back. The need to constantly keep up with what was going on, with thinking all the time, became an oppressive burden to me. As Donald told me once, "Everyone in Collins gets out of here once in a while, but you're here all the time, month after month. Are you afraid of missing something? Get out of here for a while, and I'll fill you in when you get back. Don't worry, not much is going to change when you're away."

Sometimes my mind went in the opposite direction, maybe as a way of gaining some relief, and I would tell myself I really didn't care what happened here and probably nobody else would really care either. "What was I doing in this little backward collection of shacks anyway?" I thought. I didn't want to take any more notes. I just wanted to drift into the everyday existence of village life, like everyone else, without the constant pressure to produce something of intellectual interest. Nobody else here was burdened with this task, so why was I?

It is easy under these circumstances to start feeling sorry for yourself. It took at times a considerable amount of effort and willpower to pull myself back together, to remind myself about why I was in Collins collecting all this information in the first place. To get my mind back on the right track, I concentrated on the limited time I had left and how much I still had to do. When I reminded myself that I would not have an opportunity again to live here for this extended period of time, then my motivation improved. I thought, "Other people in the village have their jobs to do, and this is just my job, to gather the information I will need to later defend my scholastic ideas." At this point I would then go on a flurry of note writing, ten or more pages a day, for the next several weeks.

Combining Research and Theory

So far in this chapter I have described the circumstances surrounding my initial research interests in Collins, my general round of daily activities, and some of the difficulties I encountered in fieldwork. I have given some idea about how I conceptualized my research task, especially in terms of viewing the data collection process as involving major areas, such as the social, economic and political worlds. I kept separate journals, mostly consisting of various facts and figures, for each of these areas. My research job as I saw it was to translate these rather specific details of life in Collins into general patterns, or "levels" of abstraction. These patterns could then be linked to theoretical arguments that have emerged during the course of other ethnographic investigations. One might think of it as moving up and down a ladder, with specific details at the bottom and highly abstract theoretical patterns at the top.

There were quite a few areas of life in Collins that interested me in an abstract sense. I have already described my interest in leadership and patron-client relations. There are also interesting aspects of Collins' social organiza-tion, such as the different bands that have merged to form the existing population and the kinship and neighbourhoods patterns that structure the village in a spatial sense. The historical context of northern First Nations life was a further dimension that I found intriguing, especially the transition from the fur trapping days to the world of the wage economy. Of course, Collins' people had only partially made this transition, which in a manner placed them between two worlds. The leap that a culture makes from an older way of life to a more "modern" setting can be sudden and dramatic, but in many of the northern communities this transition is proceeding at a much slower rate. I saw in Collins an opportunity to study in microcosm this transition between worlds, reasoning that what went on here might be pretty much the same as was going on in most other areas of the Canadian north. There was the possibility, too, that the changes Collins' people were undergoing were similar to patterns of cultural change in the so-called "Third World."

A research strategy was needed to tackle this problem. If I were to put a label on how I saw the overall picture, then it would have something to do with the interrelationships between the "subsistence resource sector" on the one hand and the wage economy on the other. Subsistence resources are the food that people are able to gather or hunt on their own, so we could also label this as "country food production." What were the characteristics of these different economic spheres and how were they merged together? Did changes in one area have corresponding repercussions in the other? In Collins, would I be able to perceive an ongoing transition from the traditional hunting economy to the wage world, or would the Ojibwa economy settle somewhere in-between?

My head was filled with such questions, especially in the beginning. What I was trying to do was develop "conceptual parameters" so that I would have some idea of the bounds of the problem. Of course these bounds were only limited by my imagination, but in order for my questions to be useful in an intellectual sense then they should be capable of providing answers to similar issues that other anthropologists have also worked on. For example, my advisor at McGill, Richard Salisbury, had conducted research during the 1950s in the New Guinea highlands among a people called the Siane. He was particularly interested in economic development issues, such as what happens when a stone age culture adopts metal tools. The book he wrote, *From Stone to Steel*, was also concerned with the wider sphere of change, such as the way leadership and political patterns were affected by an underlying economic transformation. My research in Collins should be capable of addressing the same sorts of issues that Salisbury confronted and in that way push forward our knowledge of indigenous culture change.

In the beginning of my research, I tended to see culture change in terms of two rather discrete areas. In one area was the "traditional" society, which in the northern First Nations' case, I associated with hunting, trapping and generally living the bush life. The other area was the so-called "modern" world of industrial society where one worked for wages and lived in an urban setting. The Collins' research taught me that these were not mutually exclusive areas. Native people tend to borrow from the industrial society those things, such as steel traps, guns, boats and motors, snowmobiles, cloth and metal cooking utensils, that make their life easier in the bush. They are willing to work for wages in order to obtain these items, but they do not see that this will transform them into industrialized urban dwellers. They like their life in the bush. It is the area where they feel comfortable living; they have a degree of competence in the hunting and fishing life that they do not necessarily have when working for wages. Of course there are also the matters of pride in themselves and being their own bosses, rather than having supervisors telling them what to do. The more I lived in Collins, the more I saw culture change as a long, drawn-out process, which involved many variables acting upon each other.

My major task, as I saw it, was to analyze the interrelationship between the hunting and wage work areas of northern life and the variables that connected them together. In other words I was searching for a dynamic approach, such that changes in one variable would have corresponding repercussions in an other. This search began at McGill when I was examining the ethnographic reports on research conducted on the James Bay Cree by associates of the Program in the Anthropology of Development headed by Richard Salisbury. These reports had fairly detailed information on the hunting sector of the Cree economy and on per capita income levels for three communities: Fort George, Paint Hills and Eastmain, as they were called before the area was flooded by the James Bay Project in the mid-1970s.

From the hunting data I derived figures on quantities of meat consumed per person per day and ordered these figures by community. I did the same thing with income levels, restricting them primarily to income derived from wage work. With these two rows of figures for each Cree community before me I was struck by a very odd relationship. The *higher* levels of fresh meat consumption were correlated directly with higher levels of income.

This relationship between the hunting and wage work variables completely stymied me. I thought there must be some mistake, so I checked the figures again, with the same result. The reason I was so puzzled was that our conventional wisdom would see traditional hunting and fishing activities in First Nations communities declining as people drew more income from the wage labour economy. As the reasoning would go, the more that people worked to gain a cash income, the less would be their participation in bush life activities. But according to the Cree figures, there was a positive relationship between the two variables, such that increases in earned income corresponded with *increased* hunting and fishing.

I though that I was on to an important discovery here, something that could change the way we look at northern First Nations life and something that could have important implications for government policies. But first I had to explain why this relationship existed and how widespread it might be. This is the reason why an opportunity to research such an issue in a place such as Collins, where its Ojibwa residents continued to hunt and fish, yet also earned income through the wage economy, was an important ethnographic opening for me. While I was living in Collins I would have the chance to gather the first-hand information that would allow me to make informed judgements concerning the hunting–wage work relationship. Of course it is vital to think through the theoretical possibilities and settle on a direction in one's research; it is the theory that guides the collection of ethnographic data. For an anthropologist to just record activities and gather facts or participate in ceremonies without a sense of direction or overall motive for doing so is pointless.

My approach was to tackle the problem on two fronts. The wage income side was fairly straightforward, especially in terms of the collection of the various facts and figures. In Collins, income was earned either through full-time work, such as the jobs at the CNR or the tourist lodge project at Whitewater Lake, or through part-time or seasonal forms of employment, such as guiding, trapping or making handicrafts. In order to record this material on incomes and keep track of it, I kept a separate notebook which listed all the adults in the community in one column. Over the top of the page, I listed the various forms of employment available in the community. This method allowed me to record the information already collected and note blank areas where more work was needed. My information was gathered from a variety of different sources and by using different methods. I explained to most people that I was doing research on ways to find more jobs for Collins' people, that is, I emphasized the practical application of my work. I then asked them about the sorts of work they did and the general amount of income that they earned from these activities. I use the word "activities" in the plural because most people had a variety of income-producing areas of work. Sometimes I was able to make an educated guess of a person's income, such as in the case of the railway employees. The five section men in Collins, except for the foreman, made just about the same hourly wage, so if you knew one railway worker's income, you could estimate the others'. Peter, the storekeeper, helped me a lot since he was able to give me detailed information on the production of the fur trappers, including such information as quantities of furs trapped, the different species of animals involved and the prices paid for such furs. I also had access to the records of the Ogoki River Guides organization and the wages paid out to all the workers on the Whitewater tourist lodge project.

Sometimes information on incomes came to me in entirely unexpected ways. For example, one evening, a young man, whom I recognized as one of the CNR employees, came to my door with a bunch of papers in his hand. He wanted to know if I would fill out his income tax form for him, since he heard that I was asking a lot of questions about what people in Collins were making. I invited him in and in a short time had his tax form filled out, making sure I kept notes. Actually, filling out this young man's tax form caused me an ethical dilemma. There was a matter of privacy involved here, and I probably had no right to keep track of what he made or any other information on his form. I wasn't able to satisfy myself that I was doing the right thing here, despite the apparently laudable nature of my research goals. On one side, I was pulled by my role as a researcher driven to collect the most accurate and complete information on community incomes as possible, and on the other, I was a community member doing a favour for another in a situation where there was a matter of confidentiality involved.

An even more problematical ethical issue presented itself to me some time later. I was in the habit of visiting Donald, Peter's brother and ORG boss, on a fairly regular basis. Usually I just walked in, and if he wasn't there, I waited around for a while, reading a magazine or listening to the radio until he arrived back home. On one of these occasions, I was over at the kitchen table fixing a cup of coffee when I noticed a rather large stack of papers. It wasn't the right thing to do, but out of curiosity I lifted the first few sheets off the top of the pile. I discovered a complete list of all the workers that had been employed by ORG for the preceding year, the various jobs they were on and the income they had earned. Here in a nice compete package was all the information that I had laboriously been trying to piece together over many months. Scanning this information, I realized that much of the data I had already collected through other sources, such as interviews and the like, but there was also data concerning workers that I had almost no record of. It could have been that these people were not around very much or that they were not on particularly friendly terms with me or, for whatever reason, were not likely divulge this private information to me.

Call this a form of public confession if you like, because in all these years I have never told anyone about this, but I did go through those accounts on incomes, recording those figures that were missing in my own records. I realize now that I should have asked Donald for permission, but even if he had said to go ahead, there is still the matter of the workers themselves and their right to privacy. I remember feeling an unusually intense desire to obtain this information because it would give me a very accurate record of Collins' income levels. I also remember that Donald's brother, Peter, the storekeeper, had freely given me his own business records, and so I might have presumed that Donald would do the same. Whatever the case, this is now all in the past, but the ethical or moral dimension to gathering information has been a very poignant issue with me ever since.

One side of my research, the community income levels, was now fairly complete. I was also working on the other facet—country food production. Here again, I kept a notebook in which details were recorded on the various species of animals, fish or birds that were consumed for food. Some of this information I was able to obtain through the store and my search for trappers' incomes, because meat from animals trapped was also often eaten. This was the case with beaver, for example, so that you could be pretty much assured that all of the beaver whose pelts were sold to the store were also eaten. The same probably held true for other animals, such as martin, otter and muskrat, but this was more dependent on people's individual tastes.

Most of my information was obtained in a serendipitous manner. When the pickerel were running in the spring, I talked with the men as they returned to town lugging their heavy packs of fish. How many pickerel this morning? How big? Were there other men there as well setting their nets? These questions sometimes brought about an invitation to dinner, to share in the catch. Lake trout were caught throughout most of the summer. Certain men had nets out in the lake, so I checked with them on a regular basis to find out how many fish they caught. Moose were usually hunted in the fall, although they could be shot at any time of the year, especially if they happened to wander too close to the village. People didn't store the meat, since they lacked freezers, so it was passed around the community. When I noticed this circulation of meat in the village, it was a clue for me to ask questions about who shot the moose, when and in which location.

As time went on I realized that hunting and fishing were not haphazard activities but involved what might be called a "subsistence strategy." By the term "strategy" I mean that most fish and animals are more abundant during particular times of the year, and it is during these times that they are most exploited. This occurs when fish are spawning in the spring or fall, for example. Moose are hunted once a light snow has fallen because they are more easily tracked then. Geese are also hunted in the fall, when they land in large numbers on nearby lakes while making their annual southward migration. One might say that there is a certain "maximization" procedure at work here such that country food resources are most intensely exploited during high points in the yearly cycle. Once I learned the characteristics of this cycle, I was in a much better position to collect my research material.

By the end of the year, I had managed to obtain a fairly accurate record of the total annual catch for the different animals, fish and waterfowl. For the next step in the analysis I had to do some research in biology books on the average weight of edible food for each animal, fish or bird species. To give some examples, the average moose has about 150 kg. of edible meat, bear about 85 kg. and lake trout almost 2 kg. Next I multiplied these figures by the total catch for each item. This yielded a total annual volume of edible country food of about 10,000 kg for the Collins' population. Finally, I was interested in what this was all worth in monetary terms, so, using a modest figure of $5 per kilogram, I arrived at the conclusion that the country food production total was worth about $50,000 for the Collins' economy.

When one considers that Collins' total income for the year, including earned income and transfer payments, amounted to about $220,000, then one can readily see that the products of hunting and fishing are a very important economic asset to the community. Presumably if hunting and fishing were not carried on by Collins people, then this food would have to be made up from other sources, probably from the local store, at a much greater cost than is the case with country food. In my mind, the policy-making implications of the various facts and figures that I had put together are quite significant. For example, assuming that the Collins case was typical of other northern First Nations communities, then it is highly desirable to maintain hunting as an economic endeavour in these communities. Hunting is a source of high quality protein in the peoples' diet, in contrast to the high carbohydrate diet that often results from a reliance on store-bought foods. In fact, there is considerable evidence (e.g., Szathmary et al. 1987) that a reduction in hunting is one of the major contributing factors in the escalating rates of diabetes in northern First Nations populations across Canada. My point in this exercise as it pertains to fieldwork in anthropology is to illustrate how important it is to have concrete, accurate facts if one is to make policy recommendations or argue theoretical issues. It is rather obvious to me that the credibility of one's argument is pretty much contingent upon the veracity of the evidence that one is able to marshal in its support.

Fieldwork in anthropology allows ethnographers, because they are willing to live within a community for some extended period of time, an opportunity to discover facets of human life that can be uncovered in no other way. As an example, I began this section of the chapter by describing an apparent anomaly in the relationship between income levels and fresh meat consumption in three Cree communities on James Bay. The relationship was that an increase in per capita incomes in these communities also corresponded with a rise in fresh meat consumption. Conventional wisdom would probably predict that as First Nations people became greater participants in the modern world of the waged economy, they would participate less in their traditional economic pursuits of hunting and fishing. If, in fact, First Nations people are actually hunting and fishing more, or more precisely, increasing their production of country food, while at the same time increasing activity in the wage sector, then this would certainly demand a more in-depth investigation.

In the Collins' case I used the economic statistics I had gathered to construct a series of household budgets for a range of different families depending on their income levels. I then estimated volumes of country food production for these families, in order to see what sort of relationship might exist between the two variables. The results were quite startling—as in the Cree case, higher incomes also correlated with a greater participation in hunting and fishing. The problem now was to find out why.

The solution to this puzzle was found in my notes about what individuals in each of these sample families were doing in their time off work. The section foreman for the railway, for example, spent most of his weekends and vacation times with his family away from the village hunting and fishing. He would actually hire a plane on occasion to take them to areas that were difficult to reach by conventional canoe travel. He went to these remote locations because they were under-utilized hunting and fishing areas; he was thus able to maximize his country food production for the short periods of time he had off. It was also quite noticeable that the wealthier families were better outfitted, as they had the best boats and motors, rifles, shotguns, nets, generators, chain saws and other hunting related gear. The families earning less income tended to have older, less reliable equipment in shorter supply. These families also lacked the money to hire transportation to the better hunting and fishing sites, forcing them to travel in closer proximity to the village in areas that were already over utilized, and therefore, less productive. The reason, then, why there exists a positive relationship between high incomes and high hunting output is rather obvious—country food production is maximized, not so much by the sheer time spent in such activity, but by the utilization of the most efficient equipment in areas where hunting and fishing stocks are the highest.

A conclusion such as this might not have been drawn if not for the sorts of data gathering that anthropologists do during the course of their fieldwork. It is only on the basis of long-term fieldwork that a researcher is allowed the opportunity to formulate strategies of data collection that involve a myriad of interconnected variables. Anthropologists come across insights during the course of their fieldwork that result from the day-in, day-out association with people. And most important of all, ethnographers are in a position to support their ideas using concrete figures and descriptions of events and activities that allow for a fruitful combination of fact and theory.

Experience and Fieldwork

In the quote by Clifford Geertz that begins this chapter, we are reminded that an ethnographer's knowledge is shaped by the fieldwork experience. The shapes of this knowledge are always "ineluctably local, indivisible from their instruments and encasements." As much as we like to hypothesize, philosophize or otherwise think in abstract terms, it is what goes on in our everyday life experiences in the field that shapes our intellectual reality. Whatever theoretical or ethnographic objectives we might have, they are nonetheless "welded" to everyday events and situations. We are tied in a fairly concrete manner to what happens in the social and physical settings of our fieldwork. Our theorizing serves to organize or systematize the irregularities in everyday social life. More than anything else, fieldwork is a learning experience. As with swimming or riding a bicycle, you can only know what it is like to engage in such activities by actually doing them. In fieldwork, one never knows from day to day what unexpected situations will emerge. The challenge is to profit from something we never expected to happen. If we are too rigid in our perspectives we are apt to miss significant opportunities to add to the corpus of information we seek to gather in the field.

There are two processes going on more or less at once. First, there is the day-to-day data gathering, such as my collection of country food and income statistics, that follows a pretty much set agenda. Second, there are the serendipitous discoveries that emerge unexpectedly, that may add new dimensions or viewpoints to the task. Often, though, we are not sure at the time whether to invest energy into them, as they take away from the time committed to other tasks. Two examples in my case were the young man arriving at my door wanting his income tax form filled out and the discovery of the income forms on Donald's kitchen table. While I didn't realize it at the time, both of these situations led me to rethink the ethical dimensions of data gathering in fieldwork. Without having gone through these experiences, I might never have thought through this problem or tried to resolve in my own mind what sorts of boundaries should be established during the course of my own fieldwork. In all, the personal experiences that the fieldworker goes through are perhaps the single most important factor in shaping ethnographic knowledge in anthropology.

Chapter Three

Collins: Life on the Rail-line

The fieldworker is wholly and helplessly dependent on what happens…. One must be continually prepared for anything, everything—and perhaps most devastating—for nothing. —Margaret Mead (1977)

Experience as a "Slice" of Life

In its initial writing, this chapter consisted of various descriptions of people, events and situations as they came out of my memory; after I finished with each anecdote, I proceeded with the next one that happened to come to mind. This seemed the best way to convey the nature of the fieldwork experience. Stopping to talk to people on my walks, neighbours visiting me or events happening in the village do not occur in an organized pattern. It is only later, when we have a chance to reflect on what has been going on, that we might attempt to order and organize our experiences. This brings us to my point about fieldwork. Our need, later, to systematically arrange our experiences removes them further from the "real" world. The readers, I thought, might be willing to put up with a bit of untidiness in my portrayal of life in Collins if that gave them a better appreciation of what it was actually like to be there. Maybe, also, the readers might start to make the sorts of connections in their own minds that any ethnographer would make.

The Day the Anglican Church Burned Down

"See you at church in the morning," was Peter's usual statement as we parted on Saturday nights. His wife was a church-goer, but I never saw him go, even once. I only went a few times, just to see who was there and what was going on. The minister was Anglican, and you could hardly understand him when he spoke English, but he somehow had the idea that his Ojibwa was quite comprehensible. His name was Canon Long and he had just retired to his home in Nakina with his model trains and memories of a million miles of travel up and down the CNR line from Long Lac to Sioux Lookout.

It was early in the morning and there was a tapping on my window, like a small bird pecking at seeds. "Aren't you going to church, Ed, this is a special day." There was Peter. For some reason he hardly ever came to the door, just tapped on the window. It was April, and my clothes had fallen onto the floor and were cold and stiff. I put them on as best as I could, went over to the window, and there was Peter decked out in a snowmobile helmet and goggles, as if suited up for a war.

"Look," he said, pointing in the direction of the lake.

I was astounded. The church was ablaze, with heavy smoke sifting up through the rafters and out the windows. We ran over and a small crowd was forming, standing still and silent in the snow. Some people were praying, but most watched with their mouths open.

"Let's go inside and look around," Peter beckoned, "We might be able to pick up some supplies for your cabin."

So in we went, and I noticed a propane tank in the vestibule as we went by. The scene inside was unreal. It was like standing inside a woodstove. There was not much of a sensation of heat, but the light was intense. The altar was about the only thing that I remember actually in flames, except for the woodstove which no longer had a stovepipe and was shooting flames straight up to the ceiling.

"Let's grab this rug," Peter urged, and we hauled on one end of a red carpet and pulled it out into the snow, stamping out the burning end. We went back in again and tried to pull out some pews, but the smoke was making it quite dark inside now. I remember grabbing a lighter bench near the door, but the end hit something on the way out and broke off. I went back in again and retrieved the piece. I got out just in time because the propane tank suddenly blew, sending a solid pole of white burning gas skyward.

The church disintegrated at that point, leaving bits and pieces of burning embers here and there in the snow. Peter went home and returned with his camera. Someone took a picture of us, sitting on the church bench in front of my cabin with our trophies. Peter's older brother, Donald, was sifting through the ashes, all that remained of the church, with a shovel. "Look at this," he said, motioning us over. He had been collecting the molten remnants of the chalices and candle sticks. He was quite excited, "It's real gold, you can tell." I looked down and noticed that his boots were steaming because of the hot coals he had been standing on.

The story on this whole debacle was that a new minister had arrived the night before to take Canon Long's place. His previous posting had been in the Caribbean, and so he didn't know much about woodstoves. He also didn't know that a few layers of paint and rust were about all that was holding the stovepipe together. The new minister apparently filled the stove up with jack pine, a very flammable wood, and then left for his morning coffee, feeling that in a half hour or so he would return to a cozy congregation. Instead, he and his family were making a quick retreat from the village via the Sunday morning train. What an inauspicious start, I thought. He came thousands of miles north to this Aboriginal village to spread the gospel, and in less than twenty-four hours had managed to burn their church down. No one ever saw him again.

The burning of the Anglican Church caused me to realize, some time later, that even in small, out-of-the-way places like Collins, very dramatic, unexpected events can occur. Of course there is no way, as a fieldworker, to really prepare for such situations other than to develop a sense of awareness that allows you to make the best of such opportunities. It all happened very quickly, as the burning of the church probably took no more than twenty or thirty minutes, but I learned a lot in this short time. To tell the truth, an intuitive element in me drew my attention to the people involved, rather than solely to the destruction of the building.

I was at the time puzzled by the expressions of awe or wonderment I saw on the faces of the people who were standing around the perimeter of the burning structure. Perhaps I expected expressions of horror, but, then, I too was filled with this sense of awe. After the outer wall of the church fell away, for some reason the altar remained intact. An intense white light enveloped this altar, set still with its fine linen and golden chalice. Time has a peculiar manner of appearing to slow down in such situations, as if our inner consciousness causes this to occur for dramatic effect.

Some people believe that one's true character emerges in situations of crisis. It is certainly true that Peter and I showed an astonishing lack of discretion in entering the burning church, especially with the propane tank clearly evident near the doorway. For some reason the two of us were in a playful mood, despite the danger. We acted like foolish children and almost paid with our lives.

Donald, too, showed a particular aspect of his character that morning. He didn't appear to be touched by the same sense of wonderment that captivated most of the rest of us. Instead, his behaviour was surprisingly materialistic, given the predominantly spiritual nature of the event. When Donald shouted, "It's real gold!" the mouths of the people standing around dropped in disbelief that he could be so concerned with trivia, albeit golden trivia, when there was something far more dramatic going on. But Donald was always a pragmatist, and he acted true to form that day. Peter and I, on the other hand, are pretty much dreamers at heart and not too careful about looking out for the consequences of our actions.

And what about the minister and his family, who had made such a hurried retreat from the village that morning? They must surely have been filled with intense remorse for causing the destruction of the church on their very first service in the village. I hope they didn't read into the situation an omen from the Lord that they should quit the ministry or something like that. In fact, it was probably just a matter of time before a fire in that dilapidated stove caused the building to burn down. Taken in a wider perspective, the minister and his family are just part of that group of outsiders, like school teachers, government agents and even anthropologists, who come and go in such places as Collins. Rarely, I suspect, do their activities have much of a long-term impact on the lives of the local people. The locals probably wonder why these outsiders come in the first place, what their motives are and what they hope to accomplish.

Elizabeth, who was Donald and Peter's seventy-five-year-old mother, once looked up at me and asked, "Why study Indians, anyway?" I should have had some answer, any answer, but I had nothing to say. She had a good point to make. Ultimately, I'm still not entirely sure.

Helen's Story

There is a certain routine that one eventually settles into during the course of one's fieldwork. The evenings were a time when I tried to go over the various events of the day, considering whether there was anything significant that I might have missed and should have recorded in my field notes. Since I didn't have a television or much in the way of radio either, I often had a lot of quiet time on my hands in the hours before going to bed. Many anthropologists use this time to read a novel or otherwise engage their mind in some place far away from where they are. I thought of doing this also and had brought along fiction for that purpose, but I was leery about getting too involved in novel reading. Perhaps I didn't trust myself enough. It would have been easy to while away the hours reading at night, but possibly then a fight not to pick up the novelistic adventure the next day.

At times I felt absolutely swamped with having to live this fieldwork situation all day, every day, all week, all month and so on. A break would have been nice, but I was always afraid of losing it altogether, of thinking that I didn't really know what I was doing there anyway. So, I always wanted to "keep my hand in," as they say. In the back of my mind was always the knowledge that I wouldn't be in Collins for that long, really, and that I should make the best of the opportunity. I was learning from my own experience what my own limits were and what problems I had to learn to handle. For me, fieldwork was as much about learning about me as it was learning about others. So, I felt comfortable in the evenings going over my notes or looking up things in other ethnographies, especially Robert Dunning's book on Pekangekum. In a way that was my escape. I could get away to another place and time, but the context was still somewhere in the northern bush and in another First Nations community.

Watching the train come in was a favourite pastime in Collins. People came with news about distant places and people, there was mail and baggage to toss around and in a few minutes the rumbling diesel was on its way down the tracks again. The train is the main reason why the people are here in the first place. It supplies the store with goods, allows people to move about and provides five or six permanent jobs on the Collins section crew. Every night the passenger train came in at about eleven or twelve, and I would wait up for it, but not usually go over to meet it, even though my cabin was only several hundred metres from the tracks. Most often about all I ever heard were the train's whistles, the chugging of the diesel engines and the ever quickening "click-click" as the wheels hit the spaces between the rails. I knew that most other people in the village stayed up as well. It was as if you didn't want to miss anything, even though the chances were remote that anything would ever happen at all.

On one such evening, just after the midnight train from Armstrong had pulled in, I looked out my back window towards the tracks to see about a dozen shadowy figures scurrying into the bush on their way home. I was ready to go back to my reading when I heard a light tapping on my door. A young woman, Helen, a neighbour, walked straight in and sat on the small stool beside my desk. She cupped her head in one hand and the hair flowed over the front of her face. With a waving motion she flung the tresses back, and I could tell that she'd probably had a few beers on the train. It wasn't like her to stop by for a chat.

When I first arrived in Collins, I learned that Helen's mother had just died, apparently freezing to death along the railway tracks, and as with most of these sort of deaths, there were a lot of unanswered questions. "We like you Ed," the words stumbled out, "So I want to tell you a story about coming to Collins at Christmas time." Helen seemed sad, touched with sentimentality over the bygone days with her family when she was a little girl. "We used to live out on the trapline almost all winter in those years, and us younger kids had a lot of fun. We had lots of bannock, meat and fish to eat. Dad made good money selling furs in those days."

"This was one of those better years," she continued. "I was about ten years old, and we were coming back to Collins to spend a couple of weeks there at Christmas. We had been travelling a long time, and there were two dog sleds filled to the top with furs and our belongings. All the children were piled up on top, and the sleds swayed back and forth following the ruts of the trail. Just before Collins we began to travel down the railway tracks and into that last rock cut just before town. All of a sudden Mom and Dad yelled, "Jump!" and they turned the sleds sideways over the edge of the tracks. All I remember was this big bright light of the train shining through the snowstorm and then the tangled mess of the dead dogs and everything broken up into little bits. I don't know how all of us managed to avoid getting hit by the train, but all the dogs were dead and there was nothing left of the sleds and furs. We all started to walk into town. In one moment we were happy and had everything, and the next it was all taken away. It just seems like that's the way life is around here. Well, I'll leave you alone now, Ed," and she walked back out into the night.

As I sat there, I felt a bit stunned by her recounting of days gone by. It was all too quick, it seemed to me. I wished that she would have stayed longer so I could hear more about how she felt about this childhood tragedy. It was late, but I knew that I would have trouble sleeping now, after hearing Helen's story. So I stayed up long into the night, reflecting on the apparent cruelty of life. I thought about its ironies, too. There is something about fate, if you believe in such things, that conditions us as we get older to watch out during the good times, even more so than in the bad. Just when things are going great, there is a tendency in life for the rug to get pulled out from under our feet.

Lugi

They called him "Lugi" and I never learned what it meant, but I did know that his real name was George, although he was never called that. Helen was his older sister, and Lugi, at age ten, was the youngest. I used to see him playing, like the other children, in the woods nearby, swinging in the trees, playing tag and just maintaining a constant motion. I also noticed, though, that Lugi did chores that adults do, like chopping wood or looking after his sisters' children when their mothers were away. I thought that life must be difficult for such a child, who is forced to grow up too quickly.

I liked to go for walks late at night, especially in the wintertime when the air was clear and crisp. On one of these evenings in February, I was meandering around the trails in the village. The snow was lightly falling, and I happened to notice small footprints. I followed these and they led to the schoolhouse. I pushed the door open gently, and over by the oil stove was a small child curled up. It was Lugi and he looked very peaceful. I quietly left, and back at my cabin I jotted down this poem:

> He's up all night,
> Keepin' guard,
> Tired of playin' with sleds,
> Keepin' warm in the Schoolhouse.

> First-light, & wet snow,
> Choppin wood,
> For little niece to carry,
> Keepin' warm,
> It's gotta be done.

> Papa away,
> forgotten
> that
> It's gotta be done.

I wasn't in the habit of writing poetry, but there was something about the experience of finding Lugi in the school that could only be expressed in this manner. One person, a student of mine who made comments on the manuscript, suggested that this poem is too childlike, "it takes away from the book. It seems out of place for your style. It just seems too simple and almost childlike. However, Lugi is a child and maybe this is what you are trying to portray." On the other hand, a professor friend's reaction was summed up in one word—"lovely."

I'm still not sure what it was about this experience that distressed me the way it did. Perhaps it was a certain confusion of social roles—children doing adult chores, adults acting immature in their responsibilities in life. Whatever it was, this experience caused me to reflect on the loneliness of life here. Lugi's mother had just recently died beside the railway tracks, alone and in a snowstorm. Now Lugi is forced to seek refuge from the cold and snow in the schoolhouse. Other children might be enjoying the warmth of their mother's arms, but that is something that Lugi will never feel again.

I often wondered about the way children grew up here in Collins. There were no bedtime stories at night and no "tucking in." Children might not even have their own bed, but just fall asleep wherever they can find room. I used to wonder about what sorts of adults result from this kind of childhood. However, it is also true that this is simply my middle-class values pushing their way to the surface. The way life is in Collins is just the way life is. Comparisons with other places do not help a great deal in understanding what goes on here.

At Montreal's Place

Several days before this poem about Lugi was written I had occasion to jot down a few notes concerning life in Lugi's household. Lugi's father is nicknamed "Montreal," apparently because he frequently talked about getting way from Collins and "going to Montreal," which as far as I knew, he never did. His real name was Vaino Paavola, and the story goes that he came over from Finland to work in a bush camp in the Thunder Bay area. After a while, he took up trapping, married an Ojibwa woman named Mary Basketwang and became socialized into the Ojibwa way of life. When I knew him, he could speak little English, despite having been in Canada for over thirty years, but he understood the Ojibwa language fairly well. His house was close to mine, just on the other side of the Anglican church that burnt down. His household was composed of his eldest daughter Helen, her husband Tommy, their three daughters, and Montreal's two young sons, Donald and Lugi. The following account is taken directly from my field notes, to give the reader some idea of the sorts of problems that were fairly frequent occurrences around my cabin.

Settling Domestic Quarrels, 19 February
The problem is a recurrent one at "Montreal's." Steve and Tommy quarrel, and Tommy picks on Helen who says that she will go and get Donald to protect her. This strategy incites Tommy further. Helen then seeks refuge at Peter's, but Dorothy forcibly removes her from the premises with chastisement about running over to her place every time there's trouble [Peter and Dorothy own the local store]. A short while later Montreal, also not too sober, comes over to request Peter's aid. Peter isn't home, so Montreal calls the Armstrong police—who don't show up. Apparently Helen's bleeding nose was the only injury incurred. Tommy causes ruckus at the Anglican church service. On Montreal's visit Canon Long makes no attempt to intervene but makes

the odd feeble joke. Re: Peter's comment last summer about people only interested in calling in police to settle situations that go out of control—not in seeing "justice" done. Police (one) comes on morning freight—Tommy charged—Helen pays the fine!

As it turned out, most of my field notes took this form. First, I tried to think of a title that would capture the essence, or central theme, of what I was trying to convey. The comments or observations were then jotted down in a very abbreviated form. There is not much prose or description here—as Sergeant Friday used to say on *Dragnet*, "Give me the facts, Ma'am, just the plain facts." Notice, too, that there is much information here that relates to situations only an insider in the community would know about, for example, the comments about Canon Long and something I remembered Peter saying about "justice" and the use of the police by the local people. Although the notes are sketchy, they do convey to me the essence of what I wanted to remember.

The Yellowhead Family

The Yellowhead family is one of the core centres of population in Collins. Its members originally came from Fort Hope up on the Albany river and, like so many others in this area, began to drift down towards the CNR line after WW II. Two brothers eventually settled in Collins. One, Joel, died in a house fire while I lived in Collins. He left two adult sons, Elijah and Adam, and four older daughters. The other brother was married to the former Alice Drake, who died the same year as her brother-in-law Joel. Alice had two sons, Mike and Luke, and a daughter Sally.

As foreman of the CNR section crew, Mike is one of the most successful men in Collins. He commands considerable respect in the village since he controls access to the only source of full-time employment. His income allows him a standard of living quite a bit above the norm in Collins. This income also contributes to success at hunting and fishing because of the factors discussed earlier.

Mike and his wife Nancy are also generous people. Even though they have two children of their own, they adopted two young boys when Mike's sister Sally died. In addition, they adopted two older girls, daughters of the deceased Elsie Drake. Elsie was pre-deceased by her husband Gilbert Drake. Mike's mother Alice was a Drake, but more importantly in terms of kinship connections here, Elsie was Nancy's aunt (her mother's sister) so in effect Nancy was adopting her maternal parallel cousins, who in the traditional Ojibwa kinship system would be referred to as "brother" and "sister." This all points to the necessity, of course, of sorting out all the various kinship factors in a village such as Collins before one can really grasp all the threads of the developing social relationships.

Mike's brother Luke, in contrast to Mike's favourable position in community affairs, led a troubled life. Luke was plagued with psychological problems of undetermined origin which led him to have all sorts of delusions. Many people feared him, thinking him possessed in some way. He also lived a solitary existence since he never married. When his mother died, he lost his home base and tended to just wander around the village late at night, which added to people's sense of apprehension.

Luke's cousin, Elijah, shared a similar position on the periphery of the village social order. Elijah was in his mid-twenties, had never married and lived with his married brother Adam in the home of his wife Harriet Kwandibens and her large extended family. There was a constant state of trouble between Elijah and Harriet, which added no doubt to Elijah's sense of being an unwanted outsider, living as he did with his brother's in-laws. Once Elijah came to me seeking help for a stab wound to his hand inflicted by Harriet during one of their arguments. While I was conducting my fieldwork in Collins, Elijah was killed by a passenger train outside of Armstrong while attending a "bush party." There were those who contend that Elijah was pushed onto the tracks when he was drunk by members of the Kwandibens family who lived there, but none of these allegations ever surfaced in a court of law.

I came to see the Yellowhead family as somewhat typical of the large, Aboriginal social groupings that formed the core centres of population in places like Collins. Such families have many diversified kinship links tying its many members together and also provide a series of connections through marriage with other such "clans" in the Collins area as well as "back home" at Fort Hope. Like many such families in the northern bush country, they have many unfortunate deaths, at relatively early ages, caused by things like house fires, suspected foul play. Some members are successful, the so-called "pillars of the community," while others are "hangers-on" or social misfits.

One might feel that sorting out all the family relationships is not really necessary if it does not relate in a direct sense to the main research goals or ethnographic objectives. However, I was determined to find out all I could about people's kinship and other social relationships because I regarded these as the social fabric or bedrock upon which all else was built. In Collins, people's social universe was built on kinship, and to neglect an understanding of this would have been to ignore the essence of their social life. This task of sorting out the nuances of the kinship and social universe of Collins' people was a job that began with my first days in the field, continued until the very end of the research and probably consumed as much of my effort and time as all the other various research chores combined.

In the next few pages I relate several anecdotes surrounding the unfortunate circumstance of Elijah and Luke Yellowhead and some of my further thoughts on the effects that these men have had on my understanding of social life in Collins.

Elijah's Homecoming

Elijah Yellowhead had one of those Old Testament names—like Noah, Samson, Saul and Solomon—that are fairly common in northern First Nations communities. Both his parents were deceased, and he was living with his sister-in-law's family. This arrangement was not particularly cordial, and Elijah, the introverted type, was usually the one picked on in domestic disputes. On one occasion he showed up at my door with his hand all bandaged up, apparently seeking medical attention. He'd had a fight with his brother's wife and she'd stabbed him with a kitchen knife. He had heard that I was a "doctor" of sorts. There was not much I could do for him except encourage him to clean up the wound and keep away from his in-laws.

It often struck me that Elijah was much too timid to live in such a "rough and tumble" place as Collins. Yet, this was his home, and there really wasn't any other place for him to go. It came as a shock, although not a complete surprise, when we learned that Elijah had been struck by a passenger train and killed. There was an article on this tragedy in a Thunder Bay newspaper, and I remember reading that the accident occurred in a rock cut. The engineer stopped the train and had to go out and view the gruesome scene of Elijah's body parts scattered against the rock. The passengers on the train were justifiably horrified to witness such a dreadful sight.

Details of the incident were quite sketchy. The newspaper recounts that there was apparently a small group of men engaged in an overnight drinking party. Elijah had wandered away from the group and was sitting on the railway track when the accident occurred. The story that circulated around Collins was that the other members of the drinking party were old enemies of the Yellowhead family and that Elijah had been pushed out onto the tracks, in retribution for some past incident. There was not much of an investigation, and in a few days there was hardly any mention of it. I began to keep a record of the people who had been killed on or near the CNR tracks and was surprised at the numbers involved.

People like to tell stories about the bull moose that are killed by trains. The moose sees this large creature rumbling towards him and prepares to protect his territory. The moose puts his horns down, scrapes the ground a few times with his front hoof, and begins a fatal charge into the on-coming train. It happens all the time, I'm told. It strikes me that there is an analogy here between the destructive force of modern technology and the modest attempts by nature to resist it. In telling this piteous story of the charging bull moose, I also sense that the First Nations people see themselves caught up in this onslaught of technology. Yet, too many people are killed on the railway tracks for these unfortunate accidents to be all coincidences.

Peter, the Metis storekeeper, told me once that it was his theory that the numerous deaths on the railway tracks were really a covert suicide cult. The diesel engine represents the power and destruction of white civilization over which the Native people have no control. As an act of defiance they give themselves up to the monster, not willing to live another day under its oppression. In this light, Elijah was a courageous warrior, taking a stand against the indomitable Goliath.

There were several nights in a row when Peter and I waited for Elijah's body to arrive by train. We couldn't find out where the body actually was, as there was some mix up at the funeral home, or when it was put on the train. It took about a week, but eventually Elijah came home. I remember that it was a pitch black night. The casket was hurriedly hauled from the train, hoisted onto the men's shoulders, and a strange procession wound its way through the trail in the bush. From a distance it looked sort of like a long snake carrying a box, with flashlights beaming this way and that as the casket was carried down to the Catholic Church. There were no clergy in town so the people conducted their own service, a combination of Christianity and Native spiritual elements, led by one of the village elders.

I can still picture that dark, eerie cavalcade of figures carrying Elijah's casket along the bush trail from the railway tracks. I can also remember my own feelings of ambivalence—the fieldworker part of me felt that I should get involved in the procession in some manner in order gather information, while the "ordinary person" part of me felt that this was a solemn event and that the family's privacy should be respected in their time of grief. Over the years I have spent some time reflecting on the meaning of this sense of ambivalence and what it meant to my fieldwork experience.

The event itself happened quickly, and if I was to participate in the procession and subsequent ceremony, I would have had to make a hurried decision. It was almost as if this event was one of those tests of judgement that is bound to occur sometime during one's research. As it was, Peter urged me at that crucial moment to go along and attend the service, citing what I already knew in my heart, that I would loose the opportunity to learn something significant. He also pointed out that my objections, about the family's privacy and the like, were not well founded since the people probably expected me to show up. Peter also informed me that the New Zealand engineer (who was employed on the tourist lodge project) was participating in the procession, crying and apparently caught up in the intense emotion of the event.

There is no doubt that I didn't feel the same emotion as the engineer, even though I had known Elijah for quite a few years longer. In retrospect, this is probably one of those classic fieldwork dilemmas, to get involved or not. In this case, my main regret is that my reticence about getting involved in private matters got the better of me and prevented me from becoming involved in something that could have given me considerable insight into the Collins community. I never had the same sort of opportunity again, and I regret that my own personal feelings and fears of getting involved, prevented me from doing a better research job. Even to this day, after reflecting off and on over the years on this problem, I still haven't come to any firm conclusion on this matter of social propriety and involvement.

The Second Coming of Luke Yellowhead

Luke Yellowhead was Elijah's cousin, and this whole family seemed to suffer an inordinate number of tragedies. In the spring before Elijah's death, his father Joel had burned to death in a house fire. There were rumblings in the village at the time that the fire had been deliberately set and that the door had been secured from the outside to prevent his escape. After all, how is it that he could not get out of a one room cabin that was burning down? In September, a resident of Armstrong was charged with Joel's death, but I never heard the outcome of the case. Later, with Elijah's suspicious death on the tracks, insinuations emerged again, but they were not to my knowledge reported to the authorities. Luke's mother, Alice, had also died that same year from cancer. When I returned to Montreal for several months I received the following letter from Peter:

> Well Mr. Ed, news industry being what it is I shall close on this cheerful note: two babies, no three, were born and two old people, no three died. Hilma K. had a baby. Born here. Sophie Okeese had a baby born here. Can't remember the other one. Eddie Goodwin died in Savant Lake. Seems he fell and busted his head. Joel Yellowhead died and Alice Yellowhead died. Luke keeps coming back & forth and getting progressively worse. That's good stuff Ed.
> —Love. P.

For three weeks during July and August, Luke had kept most people in the village on edge. He had escaped from the Lakehead Psychiatric Hospital in Thunder Bay and hitch-hiked back to Collins. He would roam about the village at night, probably searching for food, and then hide out in his deceased mother's abandoned cabin during the day. Every once in a while gun shots could be heard in the evening, first at one side of the village, then several hours later on the other side. These were attempts to ward off Luke's meandering around peoples' cabins. He was also spotted down at the dock trying to open drums of aviation fuel. The word was that he had resorted to "sniffing" gas, and the craziness that resulted had made the people afraid of him.

Luke was still a young man, in his early thirties at this time, and I was never made aware of the nature of his psychiatric disorder. I had known him for the five or six years as we had worked together in tree planting camps during my undergraduate days at Lakehead University. At that time, he was given to dramatic flights of imagination but was never violent. People suspected that the gas sniffing had changed this demeanour.

The situation came to a head when Donald, Peter's brother, found Luke down at the dock and confronted him. There was a plane there at the time, and the pilot had opened up one of the fuel drums to fill up his tanks. When Luke approached, the pilot locked himself in the cockpit of the plane. And when Donald came near, Luke pulled out a knife and threatened him, forcing Donald to dive off the end of the dock in order to escape.

Luke had been in and around the village for almost three weeks, but now, with this threat of violence, people's patience wore thin and the Ontario Provincial Police (OPP) were called in to apprehend him. Luke seemed to realize that he was about to be arrested, and he went "public," so to speak, by walking up and down the railway tracks in front of the village. No one dared to approach him, but for some unknown reason, I felt that I would like to renew acquaintances from our tree planting days. I walked up to him, as nonchalantly as I could under the circumstances, and greeted him with a simple, "Hi Luke, how you doing?" He acted as if there was nothing unusual in all of this, which set my mind at ease somewhat, as it would not have been out of the question for him to pull a knife on me.

When Luke reached into his jacket and struggled to pull something out, I suddenly realized that my bold approach was probably a big mistake. I froze, not wanting to create alarm by running, but what he pulled out was a piece of paper. It was a design that he had been working on for a new type of church. Luke's voice was slurred somewhat, and his eyes didn't appear quite focused, yet he was quite sincere in describing his attempt to bring the "word of God" to the people. On the paper was a drawing of a cross, which was the shape the church would have been. There was an altar at one end, with a residence for the minister in another wing. There were also what appeared to me to be incongruous elements, such as an area for a laundromat, yet this might have been tied up with his idea of "spiritual cleanliness." We talked for a while longer. Eventually the police arrived, and Luke was taken away without further incident. Luke Yellowhead died a decade later in Thunder Bay and, like some of his other relatives, under mysterious circumstances.

In terms of my fieldwork experience in Collins, the case of these two cousins, Elijah and Luke Yellowhead, posed two similar yet contrasting problems. When Elijah died I was caught up in a personal dilemma about getting involved in what I saw was essentially a private family matter, that is, Elijah's funeral. I saw this as partly a moral or ethical issue in fieldwork and partly as a methodological one concerning the "participant-observation" technique. In Luke's case there is a fieldwork issue about ethics because of his psychological problems. The question is: Is it morally right to draw a sick person into your data gathering scheme when they probably lack the ability to comprehend the data gathering situation or to give any degree of informed consent regarding their involvement? In addition, there is a related methodological problem concerning the degree to which one should jeopardize one's own safety "for the sake of science."

It is these sorts of experiences gained during the course of my fieldwork that would suggest the subtle nature of gaining information. Learning and applying a kit bag of research techniques is one matter, but under the surface there is a myriad of ethical and methodological issues that crop up quite unexpectedly in day-to-day events that require a thorough thinking through. In my mind these issues are important ones, not only at a personal level, but also in terms of the broader sphere of the "philosophy of science" and the methodological context of information management, use and control.

Sunday at Samson's

Samson Basketwang was an enigmatic personality in the village. He was a spry, elderly man in his early eighties and lived with his wife Annie at the far edge of the village. I was always amazed at how active and independent they were. In the early morning, Sam and Annie were usually out on the lake fishing for lake trout, and when they paddled close to shore their grandchildren would scamper around helping them unload their nets and fish.

On one occasion, a mid-summer's afternoon, I was out wandering through the back trails several miles from the village. My mind was off at some distant place as I roamed aimlessly here and there, picking a few flowers, smelling the scent of the pine trees in the wind and generally letting my mind float along like the clouds above. My reflections were interrupted by a loud rustling in the bush ahead of me. I sensed danger and suspected that a moose was running through the bush and that I was right in its path. The branches of the trees were very closed in at this part of the trail, forming a sort of archway, and you couldn't see any more than several metres in any direction. The noise was getting louder very quickly, and at the last second I had to dive out of the way as a large body with four rapidly moving legs came barreling down on me. As it turned out, this "creature" was Samson and Annie portaging their canoe back home from a day of fishing at some distant lake. It was amazing where they got all this energy from. They were almost running along this bush trail with quite a heavy load, a scene that would no doubt serve to inspire elderly people living down south.

The reason I found Samson enigmatic was that he always conversed in his native, Ojibwa language. This linguistic factor, in combination with his age, made him one of the less approachable individuals in the village. I was determined to change this, but wasn't sure how. On a Sunday afternoon, when the village was particularly quiet, an acquaintance with whom I was discussing this matter, pointed to a half empty case of beer over in the corner of his cabin.

"There's an ice-breaker for you. Why don't you take a few beer over to Samson's and just see what happens." I knew that an anthropologist had to make strong attempts at times to overcome all sorts of inhibitions, and, given the encouragement of my friend that everything would turn out all right, I gathered up the beer and proceeded down the path to the end of the village.

As I walked up the steps to the Basketwang's cabin I grew quite apprehensive. How would I introduce myself? How would I explain what I was doing if I didn't even speak their language? Nevertheless I was determined to go through with this—it was all part of the rite of passage of being an ethnographer, wasn't it? Surely Boas or Malinowski encountered far more difficult situations, I thought.

I tapped on the door. Annie opened it and with a broad smile welcomed me in. The inside of the cabin was neat, yet spartan in appearance. A small table was constructed under the only window. Besides a double bed and woodstove I don't remember too much else in the single room. I offered Annie the beer and she invited me to sit down with Samson at the table. He smiled, somewhat nervously. I greeted him with "*Bozho*" which was about all that I knew of the language at the time. "*Bozho*," he returned, "*Nemetabin* [sit down]," pointing to the chair.

Samson must have mistaken my feeble attempts to speak in Ojibwa as an indication that my proficiency was far greater than it was, because for the rest of the afternoon he just rambled away as he saw fit in his own language. Annie sat over on the bed, smiling all the while, as if this was "men's talk." Every once in a while she brought a tailored-made cigarette over to me, and I graciously accepted with "*Megwitch*." This was at a time when a railway strike had made tobacco of any kind rather scarce, so these custom-made smokes were a rare and valued commodity. I attempted to acknowledge this as best as I could.

To this day I am puzzled by the fact that we were able to spend a pleasant afternoon together when there was this language barrier. I now realize that this doesn't mean that there has to exist a communication barrier as well. People can pass the time together with a lot of smiles and affirmative nods, looking into each other's eyes, searching out various cues and so on. My initial uneasiness melted away with the generosity and kindness of my hosts. They made me feel welcome in their home, even though at first I felt like I was intruding on their privacy.

At one point Samson motioned that he was going outside and beckoned for me to join him. I took from this that he was going to show me where their outside toilet was. As we went around the side of the cabin I noticed all his gear—several canoes, nets stretched out, snow shoes—neatly stacked up inside the opened-ended shed. There was also the perilous sight of several large dogs jumping up at us. They were chained to a central stake and had dug numerous small pits in which to lie down all over the yard. Samson and I soon became all tangled up in the chains, dogs and holes. He fell down, and I also tripped and fell into this morass of yapping, bouncing activity. At one point I tried to hoist Samson up on my shoulders fireman style in an attempt to rescue him, but in short order we both fell back down among the dogs and tangled chains. I remember that we looked at each other, at first in disbelief that we should find ourselves in such an undignified position. Then we started to laugh at the fun we were having and at our own ineptitude.

This eighty-year-old man taught me an important lesson that day about enjoying life and about communicating with others even in the face of language and cultural differences. I had brought along a Polaroid camera and asked

Samson and Annie to stand out on the verandah of their cabin so that I could take their picture. I gave Annie a silver ring which she placed on her finger, and she proudly placed her arm across her chest with the ring shining in the sunlight. It was a Sunday afternoon to remember.

Jimmy W. Comes Home from Jail

People have long memories when it comes to crimes of violence. At times people could be willing to forgive, but seldom forget, those who have caused physical harm in the past. This is especially true for northern settlements that are isolated from law enforcement agencies. The people in such places have to develop their own mechanisms for settling disputes and dealing with the violent offender.

The thirtieth of April seemed like most other springtime days. The passenger train arrived in the middle of the day and there was the usual scurrying about with several people clambering onto the train, some getting off, mail bags and boxes being exchanged through the wide door of the baggage car, then the terse "All Aboard" as the conductor quickly pulled up the little step stool and the train chugged forward.

Fear is something you can sense, like a foul wind. No one has to tell you that there is trouble; you can feel it in the air, in the movements of the people, in the way they hurry along casting furtive glances over their shoulders. Left on the landing dock beside the tracks was a middle-aged Ojibwa man, strong in his shoulders and upper body, yet somewhat shy in his demeanour. He was obviously having quite an effect upon some of the residents, especially upon some of the older people. I was quick to start asking questions: "Who is this guy? What has he done?" I reasoned, quite rightly as it turned out, that he had done quite a bit to people in Collins at some time in the past.

Back from the tracks, along the trails and in the confines of people's cabins, there was already a steady hubbub of conversation about this man that they called Jimmy W. It also did not take me long to find out the details. Five years ago, Jimmy W. had been committed to a penitentiary for shooting, although not killing, his brother at a house party in the nearby village of Allenwater Bridge. He had also shot and mortally wounded a resident of Armstrong who had come rushing through the door of the house, but apparently he had not been prosecuted for this latter shooting. In addition, Jimmy W. shot and killed a Collins' resident, although I was never sure if this fatality resulted from the same party or had occurred at some other point in time. In any event there was sufficient evidence to convict Jimmy W. and put him in jail for a considerable period. The question on everyone's mind was "Why had he returned to Collins?" especially since there were children of his victims still living in this community.

After chatting with people in some of the small groups for a while, I went over to Peter's house. Four or five men and women were already engaged in a lively discussion around the kitchen table concerning the arrival of Jimmy W. It was as if a sort of preliminary hearing was taking place by an informal village council. Some people expressed sentiments in support of the assailant; others were quick to condemn him. I was immediately interested in the flow of the conversation as a process of judicial inquiry and an exercise in informal community decision making. Given the situation, something had to be decided in a relatively quick manner; yet the people felt that sufficient time should be spent weighing the various alternatives. A hasty and ill-informed decision, taken while the perpetrator of previous violent acts was standing outside only several hundred yards away, could have disastrous consequences.

The tenor of the discussion went as follows. First, there was a review of his general social situation, including various family and kinship connections, where these people lived then and now, and a few other comments about the victims' children, who had adopted them and so on. There was then a brief review of the case itself. What I found peculiar about this stage of "the proceedings" was that there seemed to be some general agreement on the part of the participants in the discussion as to the events as they occurred on that April night five years before. They all seemed to know who had been shot, in what order, and the various relationships among the parties involved.

There was also some general recognition as to how this account, distilled as it was from the minds of people whose own recollections of the situation must be somewhat obscured by the intervening years, differed from the "official" account that emerged during the actual court hearings. For example, Jimmy W. was convicted, from what I understand, for shooting his brother, but was not tried for (supposedly) killing one other man (from Armstrong). Yet Jimmy W. apparently also shot and killed a Collins' resident, something I was not sure figured in his conviction. The point of all this is that the participants to the discussion around the kitchen table seemed to have a pretty firm grasp of the intricacies of Jimmy W.'s case.

As to the positions people took, there were pros and cons to the argument about what to do about Jimmy W.'s impromptu arrival. I had a strange sense that he was out there awaiting a decision by the village "*panchayat,*" to use an East Indian analogy. Peter held to the "let bygones be bygones" position. Jimmy W. had committed a serious crime, that is true, but he had also served his sentence and therefore deserved a chance to rejoin society. On the other side were those apparently less charitable in their assessment. "He killed people, and their children still live here. How could he be so bold as to come back to the very place where these children live? Let him go somewhere else," they argued.

Eventually a compromise was reached, with the side pushing for compassion winning out. The decision was to offer Jimmy W. a job at the construction site of a tourist lodge about sixty miles north of the village. It was felt that, since most of the construction workers were young men, there might be some acceptance on their part of someone who had committed a crime but also served his time. However, it did not turn out this way.

The men at the construction site refused to associate with Jimmy W. They were afraid that violence could erupt, and there was little protection for them so far removed from any agency that could be called upon for help. Their reaction was to ostracize him and, by so doing, deliver the message that he wasn't welcome. The shunning process was effective. Jimmy W. asked for his own removal from the site and was last seen boarding the passenger train for Sioux Lookout.

Occasionally, I ask myself what this situation of the return of Jimmy W. tells us about the isolated, northern community. For one thing, people have a well-developed sense of self preservation. This is a practical matter for the most part since the doctors, nurses and police who might help in emergencies are too far away to be of any immediate help. People learn to rely on their intuition. In the case of Jimmy W., many felt that there was not much point in tempting fate. The old adage of "once bitten, twice shy" is a pretty general rule of social interaction given the practical realities of life in the bush, and it is hard to blame people for adopting this attitude. People who abuse their social privileges are forced to pay for their indiscretions to a degree somewhat greater than might be the conventional case in the southern, urban setting.

The sociology of group dynamics, the relationship between thought and action, and how a community goes through the process of protecting itself were all issues that I found intriguing in the Jimmy W. case. I knew from the first sight of him up at the railway tracks and from people's reactions to him that this was a situation to which I should pay particular attention. I could feel the heightened sense of anxiety in the community concerning Jimmy's arrival, even though I knew nothing about why this should cause any particular reaction. My approach was to set everything also aside and devote my attention to following this event. My first observation was that people dealt with the issue in a coherent, rational manner, despite the apparent danger in Jimmy's arrival. The matter was discussed by family members in their homes and by the community's leaders.

The people in Collins, I sensed, were trying to get a hold on their anxiety. They did not immediately jump out, for example, and take some rash action like forming a mob or vigilante group. I also sensed that I was witnessing a historical and cultural way that people in this bush village dealt with crisis, a way that had been handed down through the generations. As in the past, they couldn't rely on some outside power to deal with this issue for them. They didn't physically threaten Jimmy in any way or attempt to coerce him to leave their village. Perhaps they feared a violent outburst on his part and thought better of following this course of action.

The situation reminds me somewhat of what has been happening recently in the larger Canadian society when a sex offender is released from jail. People are demanding to know the address of the offender and the conditions of his release, and the police are complying with these requests, even though the release of such information would appear to contravene the offender's civil rights. One might argue that, where there is a potential threat to personal safety, a certain restriction on the offender's civil rights is a justified action. I would suggest that in places such as Collins, which are removed to some extent from the influences of the Canadian justice system, that people will activate their own social and cultural mechanisms for dealing with community threats. Their choice of action was one of passive resistance or "shunning." People regarded Jimmy's arrival as a serious situation that had to be dealt with. The possible consequences of letting him just settle into the community were all too much of a risk for Collins people to take on. It was this coming together in the face of a significant social threat and the subsequent maneuvering by the townspeople to mitigate the possible negative consequences of this threat that I found most interesting about Jimmy's arrival that day.

Alfred the Goat

Domesticated animals, aside from dogs, are usually quite a novelty in the north. My brother, a former schoolteacher in Collins, had taken up farming on a small scale outside of Thunder Bay and thought that goats could make a unique contribution to Collins' food supply. Goats are usually hardy animals and, the reasoning went, would be well suited to foraging around the village as they don't require any special source of food, at least in summer. The main reason for bringing in goats was that Collins is a community with a large population of children who don't have a regular supply of fresh milk. The idea was to initiate the experiment with a single goat and see how that worked out.

The first goat was hand delivered in the middle of summer. As soon as it was brought off the train, the goat became a favourite among the children, who named their "pet" Alfred. (Everyone thought of Alfred as a male despite the rather obvious biological signs to the contrary). Alfred was given free rein in the village. Generally the dogs were wary of her, as they had not seen a goat before, and Alfred could make all kinds of strange noises and shake her small horns in a menacing fashion.

Several of the children were given the task of milking Alfred on a regular basis. I even took a turn at it myself. The milk required no special separation or other procedures, and about all that needed doing was to pick out the goat hairs and cool it in the store's deep freeze. The fresh milk was a welcome addition to the diet, relished by young and old. Alfred roamed about the village for the rest of the summer, and as I returned to Montreal for the fall, that was the last I saw of her.

Upon my return after the Christmas holidays, one of my first questions concerned Alfred. "How did she make out during the winter, so far?" I asked. People looked down at the question, so I knew she must have met a sorry end. I had visions of Alfred being attacked by vicious dogs or just wandering off aimlessly into the dense bush surrounding the village, never to be seen again. But no, that was not what had happened. It was nighttime, but one of the fellows took me out behind Peter's house. I remember that the January weather was particularly cold that year, and the snow glistened in the moonlight, as it swirled up in funnel-shaped formations. There were several old sheds out back. One of the larger ones had been Alfred's home for the winter, but it was hardly ample protection from the frigid wind. My guide swung open the door on the smallest building. It was crammed with various odds and ends. There were sheets of plywood and other flat objects placed on the shelves. He reached up to the top of the storage area and began to tug on something. Soon it was apparent to me that these were Alfred's legs, and in short order he pulled the goat out and stood it upright in the snow, adjusting it slightly, presumably so that the animal would have the correct posture. Its eyes stared up at me, and I thought it such a cruel fate that Alfred should pass away in this fashion, so lonely and cold. The man quickly slid Alfred back onto her resting place, kicked aside some snow blocking the door, and explained, "Alfred just froze solid, standing up in the barn over there. There wasn't much we could do about it except put her in this shed. The ground is too hard to bury her, and no one would think of eating Alfred." That was the last of the goat experiment.

Messages from the Past

There was a large field in front of my cabin. The trading store and house were directly across from me, and the whole area was surrounded by tall jack pine. In the winter, when the wind blew across this field, the snow whirled up in strange cone shapes, and the wind blowing through the needles of the pine trees made a peculiar, eerie noise that I have heard with no other type of tree.

It was my habit in the evening to go for a stroll after supper, to get some fresh air and try to clear my head from the smell of fuel oil in my cabin. On one of these occasions just by chance I noticed a small piece of paper skimming across the snow, gayfully darting this way and that, then resting for a few seconds before shooting away again. Having nothing much better to do, I began to chase this elusive slip of paper, which was behaving like a scared rabbit. Finally, I managed to snare my quarry, and to my amazement it was a page from a storekeeper's account book dated August 16, 1950.

The heading on the bill was "Jas. Haverluck, fur buyer and tourist outfitter." It looked like part of an order for the fall trapping season. The prices were rather low by today's standards—24 lbs. of flour for $1.75, 5 lbs. of sugar for $.65, 3 yds. of cloth for $1.00 and so on. I felt that I had established some strange link with the past, but where could the bill have come from?

As time went on, I found many more of these bills blowing around on a windy day in the vicinity of the cabin. After a while, I made a point of going for walks when the wind blew up to see if more of these "messages from the past" would be delivered my way. To me these were an historical resource. Most of the bills were from the early fall of 1950, and I thought that the information in these bills could be used to learn something about the past social and economic characteristics of the community. Each bill indicated the purchaser's name, the date and the items bought, and from these I developed a profile of the occupants of the village in 1950 and gleaned indications of such things as household budgets and reliance on store goods.

It was not until the next summer that I discovered the source of these bills. There was an old storage shed beside the store that was built up on stilts, probably designed to keep out predators. The place was cluttered with old flour sacks and other paraphernalia from by-gone days. Out of curiosity, I began to rummage through this stuff one day and discovered at the very back of the room a cache of old papers and account books, as well as a small pile of loose bills of the same sort I had been finding. There was also a crack in the floor near where the bills were situated, and it looks like whenever a strong wind blew across the area, it drew out a few of these bills and sent them scurrying across the field in front of my cabin.

The lesson for me here is that you never know when useful information will be presented to you or by which means. Do not throw anything out or consider it irrelevant because you just never know what will turn up next. From all these bills put together I was able to construct a fairly accurate socio-economic profile of the Collins community at a pivotal time, just before the fur trade economy began to go into sharp decline. I also was able to learn about the way people moved about from place to place along the rail-line and about those people who had stayed in one place for long periods of time. I still have these bills tucked away in my office, and I am pretty sure that in the future they will continue to be of considerable historical interest.

The Fur Trader's Puzzle

Shortly after the discovery of the account bills in the storage shed, I was again rooting around, this time in a back office of the store. I pulled out a dusty bookcase and found an old account book that had fallen behind the shelf. I asked Peter if I could borrow it for a while and hurried home with my new-found treasure.

On top of the first page was written R.R. Ratcliffe, Nov 2/40–May 3/41. The accounts were written in elegant penmanship of the sort never seen today. In all, there were about twenty pages. On each page, various columns were set out, indicating the date of a transaction, the person's name, the address, furs bought, and price paid. I knew right away that I had made another important discovery. Here was a list of all the people who had come into the Collins store over the 1940–41 trapping season. I could reconstruct population movements, availability of fur-bearing animals, and in general, the economics of the war-time fur trade industry. All of this information could be compiled according to the trapper's community of origin, various other relatives and friends they travelled with, and possible economic strategies (only small amounts of furs tended to be traded at any one time).

I spent several weeks putting this information together and was able eventually to discover some general patterns. For example, many of the trappers coming to the rail-line trading store were from locations much farther north in the Albany River area, such as Fort Hope, Ogoki and Lansdowne House. The trappers probably brought small amounts of fur with them to be used as "spending money" on their excursions down to the rail-line to visit relatives and friends. I also discovered that many of the trappers, such as Ombabika, Kowkash, Ferland and Kagmagami, listed as resident in the rail-line locations, had the same surnames as those trappers from the more northerly posts.

What I read into this was that many of the trappers had already moved to the rail-line locations on a semi-permanent basis, and so they acted as a sort of vanguard of a general north-to-south movement of trapping families during the war years. This was also the time when a number of trading stores were just being opened along the rail-line, and they generally paid higher prices for furs than the Hudson's Bay Company stores in more remote northerly locations. Not only were fur prices high, but store-bought goods cost less as well, so there were strong economic incentives for trappers to trade furs along the rail-line.

The opening up of a new transportation facility through northwestern Ontario, such as the CNR line, had far reaching effects on the First Nations populations in the area and on the fur trade economy in general. The railway allowed a distinct economic advantage for the independent fur traders along the rail-line over their Hudson's Bay Company (HBC) competitors to the north. Most of the HBC goods were still brought in from England by ship and then hauled down the various river systems, such as the Albany and Attawapiskat, at considerable cost. The Native people were astute enough to realize that the profits of their own trapping enterprises could be increased by taking advantage of the cost differentials involved.

This analysis no doubt involved a certain amount of extrapolation on my part, but I have nonetheless found that this single account book was an invaluable aid in reconstructing an earlier phase of the Collins community, and indeed, of many other First Nations communities in this area of Ontario. Important demographic and economic shifts were occurring during the war years, and this account book allowed my study to rest on very concrete and detailed information that would have been be available from no other source. Again, it was this sort of serendipitous discovery that opened new avenues for my investigation. Now to the interesting part.

For whatever reason, the fur trader, Mr. R.R. Ratcliffe, wrote part of his accounts in a peculiar code. On the facing page is a copy of the first several pages of his account book:

For those who like to solve puzzles, I hope there is enough information here to break the fur trader's code. The task is to discover which numbers the various letters stand for. The task is not as straightforward as one might think. The main complicating factor is that furs are graded differently depending on their

Furs Bought 1940–41 Season

Nov.	2	Old Mrs Yapul	Ombabika	Squirrels	2.10	42
	2	"	"	Ermine	DO	2
	4	Wilfred Fournier	"	Mink	OKK	1
	4	"	"	Ermine	EO	1
	4	"	"	Squirrel	RO	3
	6	Mrs Calhknis	"	Mink	W.KK	1
	6	"	"	Ermine	OK	2
	6	"	"	Squirrel	.EO	5
	6	"	"	"	.EO	5
	8	John Head	"	Ermine	.DO	2
	8	"	"	Mink	EK.KK	2
	8	"	"	Ermine	DK	1
	8	"	"	Squirrel	O	1
	14	Wilfred Fournier	"	Otter	RO.KK	2
	14	"	"	Mink	W.LK	4
	14	Old Somcuse	"	Otter	C.KK	1
	14	Roy Yapul	"	Otter	RO.KK	2
	14	"	"	Ermine	.EO	1
	15	Mrs Wm Johnson	"	Mink	IKK	1
	15	"	"	Squirrel	DO	7
	15	"	"	Ermine	DO	1
	16	Howard Linklater	"	Mink	CK.KK	5
	16	"	"	Squirrel	DO	15
	16	"	"	Ermine	R.WO	8
	20	Mrs Calhknis	"	Mink	R.KK	1
	20	"	"	Squirrel	.RO	5
	20	"	"	Ermine	RDO	6
	20	Joe Matinas	Ferland	Otter	EI.KK	2
	20	"	"	Mink	OW.KK	8
	20	"	"	Martin	EK.KK	1
	20	Wilfred Fournier	Ombabika	Mink	EW.KK	5
	20	"	"	Otter	RO.KK	1
	20	"	"	Squirrel	RK	3
	20	"	"	Ermine	MK	3
	22	Jimmy Kwissis	"	Otter	EC.KK	2
	22	Michael Skubik	Kowkash	Mink	?	?
	22	"	"	Otter	L.KK	?
	22	"	"	Ermine	DK	1
	22	"	"	Squirrel	—	1
	22	"	"	Reds	D.KK	1
	26	Wilfred Drake	Kagmagami	Mink	RO.KK	2
	26	"	"	Ermine	.OK	2
	26	"	"	Squirrel	.RO	4
	26	"	"	Mink	CC.OK	7
	26	"	"	Ermine	R.OK	6
	26	"	"	Squirrel	O5	1
	27	Shipped				
		Cost CDM.WK				
		Sold DLW.WO				

quality, so that five ermine, for example, brought in one day would not be worth the same value as the same number of ermine brought in at some other time. As to why Mr. Ratcliffe used this code, we can only guess. Probably he wanted to keep his accounts a secret from inquisitive employees, but there could be other factors involved, such as possible searches by game wardens or tax and income implications that he wanted to keep to himself. There is intrigue out there in the backwoods, so have some fun with the fur trader's puzzle. (The answer can be found at the end of this chapter.)

The Collins Experience

One of the problems with fieldwork is that we never seem to have as much control over what is going on around us as we would like. Perhaps we have the most control in structured interviews, but when it comes to most of the techniques available to an ethnographer, such as participant observation, we pretty much have to go along with the flow of events around us. It is a matter somewhat of how much we would like to shape events and how much we are willing to let events shape us.

In the field we are "wholly and helplessly" dependent on what happens, to use Margaret Mead's words. There was not much that happened in Collins that I did not find interesting in one manner or another. This does not mean that I tried to force all my experiences into the mould of my political-economic theme, but I played around with situations long enough in my mind to see if I could take advantage of them in some way for research purposes. I never forgot that I needed material.

Fieldworkers need particular events and situations in order that they may be studied, analyzed and placed in a larger context. As Hortense Powdermaker explains, anthropologists "write out of their immersion and participation in a particular situation from which they have been able to detach themselves. But they write of the particular ... the particular illuminates the human condition" (1966: 296). Sometimes these "particulars" come to us, unannounced, on our doorstep, but mostly we have to go out and seek them, to reach out, even though we may feel shy and retiring.

The little "snippets of time" that are recorded in this chapter illustrate in so many ways, the situations and opportunities faced by most fieldworkers. I believe that I now have some understanding of what Geertz meant when he talked about ethnography becoming "imprisoned in the immediacy of its own detail" (1973: 24). Take, for example, "Helen's Story." My recollection is that I felt quite uncomfortable with her visit. It was late at night, and the prospect of her crying and going on for some time about her life's problems was something that I wasn't prepared for at that late hour. Yet, as Helen recounted tales of her childhood, especially the harrowing experience when her family's dog sleds were hit by the freight train in the rock cut, I found that I was becoming fascinated with the tragic circumstances of her life. As it turned out, this was the only time she ever visited me, and we never had any more than a few words of conversation from that point on.

It is almost as if time becomes crystallized at certain points in our fieldwork journey, such that some events attain added meaning or significance because they stand out in such sharp relief to the other mundane things that are going on. I felt that this was especially true with the episode about the Anglican church burning down. The inside of the church glowing in a super white light, with the neat little altar covered with clean linen and adorned with golden candlesticks, as yet untouched by the flames surging up from the decrepit woodstove, was an unforgettable sight. I knew that I was in an extremely dangerous situation, standing inside this burning inferno, with its volatile propane tank nearby, but there was a certain fascination with the moment. It was as if I were straddling two worlds—the here and the beyond—and I wanted to enjoy, even for a few fleeting seconds, the power and majesty of it all. There was also the rapidity of the burning, which turned everything, moments before so white and beautiful, black, charred and filthy. And to see Donald digging around, turning up little bits of molten chalices and candlesticks, was a snap back to reality—a reality where people grub around for what they can get.

There were other times, too, when I should have recoiled from danger but nonetheless was drawn inexorably forward. The sight of Luke Yellowhead, for example, sauntering back and forth along the railway tracks, out in full view of a very concerned village populace, was one of those situations. It had only been the night before that people were firing warning shots his way, to scare him off. Luke also had pulled a knife on Donald down at the dock and trapped a terrified bush pilot in his plane. But here I was, with all this "anthropological bravado" behind me, strolling up to have a chat with him. When I got close enough to him to see the deranged look in his eyes, I knew that I had no business being where I was. Yet I had passed the point of no return; there was no opportunity for me to run away and still save face, so I just mustered up as much courage as I could by trying to conduct a little interview. The lesson for me is that there are certainly limits to the extent that one should go to collect data, and putting your life in danger isn't one of them. I also felt a bit sheepish, when I thought about it later, with my "show-offy" approach to this situation, when I should have exercised much more discretion.

It is in hindsight that we learn from our experiences in fieldwork, but a certain period of reflection is necessary at times to consider the direction our fieldwork is heading and what we should be doing to keep it on track. Despite our well thought out hypotheses, so carefully studied in the library beforehand, and with a methodology that will surely yield answers to the questions we have deemed are of considerable scholarly importance, we learn that we must struggle with how little control we actually have over our fieldwork. The people, places and things that we become "encased" in are not often what we would have predicted or maybe even preferred. We really have no choice but to play the cards, as it were, that are dealt to us. It's up to us to make of them what we can.

Slips of yellowed paper buffeted by the wind across a snowy field, a couple of beers with an elderly couple who speak no English, a child's footsteps through the early morning snowfall, encounters with a crazy man—what are we to do with all of these experiences? They didn't readily fit into my theoretical initiative about "economic development and political change," but I found such situations too interesting in their own right to just forget about. They are the everyday stuff of life—the details, background and personalities that fill out our life's experiences, imbue them with meaning, however obscure, and serve to propel us forward in time.

Answer to the fur trader's puzzle:

The ten numbers, 1 to 0, in the fur prices column correspond to the letters "RED COW MILK."

Chapter Four

Armstrong: A CNR Town

Fieldwork or participant observation has led many anthropologists to struggle with epistemological problems related to understanding other cultures as part of a dialectical process of self-understanding. —Robert Ulin (1984: xi)

Armstrong

The town of Armstrong is not much more than a strip of dusty road with the CNR and OPP stations on one side and a few stores and houses on the other. About three hundred or so people live here on a full-time basis, but in the summertime, an influx of tourist operators and American visitors gives the impression of several thousand. However, tourists actually don't spend much time in Armstrong as they are quickly whisked off by float plane to one of the numerous "fly-in" operations in the area. The core of the town's population is composed of First Nations people, comprising Metis and non-status and status "Indians," who have moved to town from one of the surrounding reserves. Jobs for this population in Armstrong are not very plentiful. The Canadian National Railway employs some men on a year-round basis on the section crews and others in the summer months for track repair and maintenance work. The tourist operators hire Native men to work as guides in the fly-in camps and sometimes their wives as cooks. There is also a Ministry of Natural Resources base that occasionally employs First Nations people, almost always to fight forest fires. Employment Insurance and other transfer payments round out most families' incomes.

Armstrong's history as a settlement didn't really begin until the 1950s when the Canadian and American armed forces built a radar base here. It was all part of the DEW (Distant Early Warning) line scheme during the Cold War era. The idea was to detect Russian missiles, but such a detection centre practically on the southern border of Canada could hardly have helped in the event of a nuclear attack. Millions of dollars were spent on the base, but the soldiers mostly kept to themselves. By the 1960s, with the era of satellite technology, the base had out-lived its usefulness. Everything of any use was carted away, and the buildings were left to the "Armstrong Development Committee" to use as a motel, restaurant and garage.

In the local dialect, the "K.G." means the King George Hotel, which is a rather regal banner for such a run-down establishment. The K.G. is situated directly across the street from the OPP headquarters, and since the latter was constructed well after the former, one can only assume that there was some strategic intent in locating the police station across from the town's main watering hole. It certainly facilitates any arrests for intoxication that have to be made. Right about closing time, several officers drive across the street. There is an abnormally high set of stairs in front of the K.G. that serves as a sort of inebriate test. Anyone tumbling down the stairs is presumed to be "intoxicated in a public place." This local arrangement is apt to suit everyone concerned, since the ill-fated patron is not likely to have a place to sleep. And, as far as the police are concerned, placing such people in jail means they don't have to worry about them causing trouble during the night. Charges are not usually laid in these cases, and the lock-ups are left to trundle off to the restaurant down the street in the morning.

On the few times that I actually stayed overnight in Armstrong, I usually spent the night with Peter's mother, Elizabeth, who told me that I could stay there even if she wasn't home. On one such occasion, I remember settling into her place for the evening. It was winter, and deadly cold outside, but the oil stove gave off a lot of heat. I had made a pot of tea and thought I would take a breather outside to look at the stars. I wondered around for a few minutes, but without my overcoat, I was soon anxious to scamper back inside. To my amazement the door had somehow become locked. The latch must have closed when the door banged shut. I peered inside, longingly staring at my hot cup of tea and the warm glow of lights in the kitchen. I was almost ready to panic. You can't stay outside long in weather like this without freezing. I found an old shovel and waded around to the back of the house in waist-high snow, but failed in my attempt to pry open a bedroom window.

As luck would have it, an OPP officer lived next door, but I was hesitant about calling on him in case the locals might think I was collaborating with the law. The officer's large German shepherd was barking and jumping up and down on the end of its chain. But as the dog couldn't quite reach the door, I began to knock, at first timidly and then loudly in desperation. The officer came to the door, listened to my story and began to cut up an old plastic Javex bottle. "You best look the other way," he cautioned, "you could call this a trade secret." With a flick of the wrist he had the latch open. He muttered something about "a bitch of a night" and scurried back into his house, leaving his dog to continue its pitiful harangue. Before going to bed that night, I reflected on the need to exercise a bit of caution once in a while.

Only once did I have occasion to stay at the K.G. I had just got off the train from Collins and must have looked rather grubby. I wore a beard at the time and had long bushy hair. My constant companion was a large pack-sack that I had retrieved out of the trunk of one of my dad's used cars. My appearance didn't impress the owner of the hotel, who promptly informed me that there were no rooms available, although it didn't appear to me that the hotel was full of guests. I pleaded that there was no other place to stay in town. I then explained that I was a student from McGill University in Montreal conducting doctoral research in the area. His ears perked up at this, probably thinking that I was working for the Ministry of Natural Resources for the summer, and on that account was allowed to look like a slob. I then added that there was a whole party of researchers coming to Armstrong soon, who be needing accommodations, and that I was their advance scout. The ploy worked and I was given a room in which to stay.

I remember climbing the stairs and feeling disgusted with myself for my lack of independence and for having had to grovel. I noticed that there was only one other room occupied, by a young mom and her two children. However, I was glad for the chance to get cleaned up and have a temporary reprieve from the wood smoke, outhouses and fly bites. This was an ideal time to write up some of my field notes, and so I propped my knees up on the bed in a sort of desk. It was then that I spotted a large rope coiled up under the window. It was secured to the hot water radiator, and I imagine in the case of a fire in the hotel the patrons were supposed to hurl this rope outside as a makeshift fire escape. I shuddered at the thought at how quickly this old frame building would burn down and how futile would be one's attempt at escape, rope or no rope.

The next morning I made my way across the street to the train station and was surprised to find the door to the waiting room was locked tight, despite the posted hours of "9 am to 4 pm." There was also apparently no way of finding out about the arrival and departure times, as I could not see a bulletin board through the window. In any event, the coming and going of the trains depended pretty much on where it might be held up along the two-thousand-mile stretch between Vancouver and here, so you needed some inside information anyway. There were five or six Native people milling about outside the station who would probably wait there all day for the train, if necessary, rather than risk the embarrassment of a confrontation with the white train personnel.

I found it hard to believe that such forms of covert discrimination still existed. It made me think of a postcard that a fellow student had shown me of a bar in South Dakota with a sign painted above the entrance, "No Indians Allowed." I wandered around to the back entrance that the employees use, thinking that here should be a sign posted, "Whites Only Allowed," just in case any Native should saunter in by mistake. Inside, a conductor was joking with a yard employee, and another man was tapping feverishly on his typewriter keys. It didn't take long to find out that the "Number 1 passenger," the westbound train, was due shortly. When I asked about the locked door to the waiting room, the yardman remarked that "We don't want this riffraff [meaning Native people?] hanging about the station bothering us. We usually open up the wicket for ticket sales about ten or fifteen minutes before the train is due anyway, so there's no harm done, right?" I was going to ask about how a person was able to find out when the train was due in the first place, since there was no public posting of these times, but decided to drop the subject.

It was somewhat of a surprise, then that just before the train's arrival, the station area quickly filled up with people. I later learned that an informal communication system was at work and that the train times were discussed all day long. People often found out about the train times from friends or relatives who were CNR employees. You could overhear parts of these conversations: "There was a wreck of a freight on the siding at Wagaming. They'll have it straightened up in about an hour," or "The Number 2 was held up for half an hour by a section crew at Ferland."

There was another "trick" that the veterans used and which I employed with considerable success. There were telephone boxes situated at periodic intervals along the railway tracks for use by the railway employees. These phones provided a direct line to the station, and if you called up and talked in the jargon of the track hand (always calling trains by their number and never referring to a train as a train) you could usually get the most accurate information available. This information could then be spun out to eager listeners, who were forced to be polite and engage in a code of deference in order to get these valued tidbits.

Linguistic Tidbits

It seems like most of the town comes out to greet the train, as if there isn't much else worthwhile to do. I noticed a group of three or four Ojibwa teenage boys carrying on a conversation with several white girls on the train. The boys said that they were going to teach then "a little Indian." When the train departed, the girls waved enthusiastically, shouting what they thought was a farewell greeting, "*Pejogin, pejogin.*" I was slightly embarrassed to hear this myself, since in the Ojibwa language, "*pejogin*" means penis. This was knee-slapping humour as far as the teenage boys were concerned. The same sort of linguistic mix up can sometimes occur unintentionally. I once heard about a girl from Gull Bay by the name of Maureen. The local Catholic priest used to call her "Mo" for short. At every instance she would blush but did not want to correct the priest. Finally, she could take it no more and informed him that in Ojibwa the word "*mo*" means "feces."

The Ojibwa word for the train is "*scutee taban.*" "Scutee" means fire and "taban" is the northern Ontario variant of the Algonquian word "toboggan." So train means, literally, "fire sled," which I thought was a pretty good description of the old coal-fed locomotives, with their cow catchers and billowing smoke stacks. The Ojibwa call themselves "*Anishenabe,*" meaning "the people." A person is also sometimes called "*In-in-i,*" which can be found in such interesting terms as "*Tea-K-Inini,*" which is the word for a person of Asian descent. This literally means "Tea man." I am not quite sure what the "K" letter stands for but suspect it is simply what you might call a linguistic filler or bridging mechanism which serves to separate two vowels.

In most normal discourse, the Anishenabe refer to white people as "*wab-skeyweyas,*" literally "white-meat." I never regarded the term as particularly flattering. Similarly, Blacks are referred to as "*makadey-weyas.*" There are also certain terms that refer to nationality, such as "*Shaganash*" for Englishmen.

There are actually a lot of terms used to refer to white people to do with the different roles they play in the lives of the Ojibwa. A storekeeper, for example, is called "*okima*," meaning "boss," since in northern communities, these were usually powerful people, responsible for extending credit for the trapping season, buying furs and, later, dispensing welfare. A variant of this is "*amik-okima*," or "beaver boss," for the game warden who gives out the fur tokens and decides on the quotas for the various traplines. There was also the "*shonias-okima*," or "money-boss," for the welfare officer.

The Anishenabe call their own elected chiefs "*okima-khan*," which is a peculiar term meaning "like a chief, but not quite." The idea is that this is a chief in name only, not like the real or powerful bosses like the Hudson Bay Company fur traders. There is a similar instance of this in the term for the wooden decoys that are used to attract ducks and geese in the hunting season. The decoy is called "*sheeship-khan*," which is to say, "looking like a duck, but a mock-up of the real thing, a pretense, a sham of sorts."

A term that I heard quite a bit on the construction site was "*umtegoshee-causo*," which means literally, "to act like a white man." The reference here is to Ojibwa men who were placed in positions of authority but who started to act "pushy—like a white boss." This reminded me of a similar phrase that I read about in Ruth Landes' book, *The Ojibwa Woman*, in which she describes the vision quest among the youth as "*manitou-kauso*," which is to say, "to act like the gods or spirits."

It seems like just about everybody has some sort of Ojibwa nickname. I heard myself called by several names, the most common of which was "*mistoon-ance*," which means "little beard or mustache." The suffix "ance" is, I believe, what the linguists call a diminutive, which is to say, something smaller than the original. For example, another name I was sometimes called was "*semanse*," or "little cigarette." This is in reference to my propensity to roll abnormally small smokes as a way of conserving tobacco. As the idea of conserving in some people's mind is quite close to the idea of hoarding, there is a pejorative connotation, albeit a small one, here as well.

A Tinge of Sarcasm

The name "*mistoon-ance*," or the reference to "*umptegoshee-causo*," have a certain tinge of sarcasm associated with them that I find pervades people's way of talking about others. There is also a curious sense of humour, as in the name, "*mons-skish*," meaning "moose nose," used in reference to one of Collins' main leaders (Donald). The following letter from Mons-skish's brother sent to me from Collins when I made a trip back to Montreal helps to illustrate the humour-sarcasm aspect of the local psyche. It was written at a time when there was considerable negotiations going on between Collins' leaders and a government agency called ARDA (Agricultural Rehabilitation and Development Agency) over the terms for the funding of the Whitewater project.

> January 7th
> Dear Mr. Ed:
>
> To-day I thought would be a good time to answer your letter of the 14th of September last. Dorothy took the children back to Winnipeg so am sitting here with really not a hell of lot to do for a change. It is really nice to be alone to think and meditate what with my usual busy schedule and all.
>
> I trust M. Claus was good to you on the 25th and showered you with gifts of all description. I took the liberty of writing a letter to him for you and telling of all your good deeds to mankind. I wonder if he took the letter at face value. If not, well, maybe next Christmas I won't lay it on so thick. But surely he gave you a new pack sack. You at least deserve that.
>
> I had a few letters from Bill the hippy and I gather he, well, sort of likes it up there. Maybe his trip to Mexico will make up for any hardships suffered now.
>
> The Whitewater Wilderness Lodge Project has ground to a halt as of Oct. 30th but will try to so some winter building starting this week. Seems to be some doubt as to whether a log can be peeled in the dead of winter, we shall see soon. I myself have never tried to do this but sure hope logs are peelable then.
>
> Say, how are you doing on that book on Donald? I, and others, believe it should be worth a Nobel or whatever that other prize for literature is, at the very least considering the subject. Seriously I hope you are completing a masterpiece. We have started on the Armstrong Project, and it seems to be moving along quite nicely. I suspect already maybe we might be losing again but I always am of that nature. At this stage we can only hope as a lot counts on how Armstrong accepts our ingenious and ingenuous plan. The Provincial Government so far likes it but it is going to cost a few dollars.
> All the Best,
> Peter

The Armstrong Project referred to in this letter was a Collins' scheme for turning the old radar base into a furniture factory. The originators of this plan reasoned that since there were already buildings to work in, plus equipment such as generators and so on, that this would be a good way to develop employment opportunities. In the end, though, almost everything of value at the base was sold by the provincial government to a salvage company, which cleared it all out in a matter of days. The history of Armstrong has been like that;

the plans for the village have been grandiose at times, but like King George himself, in time their importance is eventually forgotten. Nobody in Armstrong ever knew why they were supposed to be afraid of the Russians in the first place. This is a peculiar aspect of the Canadian north. There are these grand images, of an endless wilderness for one, that seem to attract improbable pipe dreams, like a paranoid radar base. No wonder the locals see the outsiders as inscrutable foreigners.

Fieldnotes—Armstrong Station, 15 Feb.
The Scene: Waiting for #1. Couple of train men and women (all white) in discussion:
"Well from what I hear it's belly-up. Yah, that project. They're only minor politicians, not the business men that old Jock (Peter's father) was. Why, he made things run—like the store for instance—there's nothing there now.
And how 'bout this bus-line. Took a big grant I hear. I'm very sceptical that they can make a go of it."
Conductor (waiting for the train).
C: "You're going to Collins aren't you?—yes" [pause].
C: "What do you think should be done down there?"
Me: "About what?"
C: "The store, for instance!"
Me: "It's difficult to run a store when there's not much revenue coming in."
C: "Well I'll tell you what should be done. Give them all a case of wine and hunting knives—end of problem."
Me: "You mean you prefer genocide? "

Ethnic Tension Causes Stress in Fieldwork

Travel along the Canadian National Railway is a fact of life for the people of this section of Northwestern Ontario. Travel by train is a convenient means of transport in so many ways; it costs only pennies compared to hiring a plane, and it takes only a fraction of the time that it would take by boat and motor. Yet, there are drawbacks and difficulties of a larger magnitude.

Life on the rail-line involves a degree of prejudice that First Nations people are forced to cope with. The railroad, as a social institution, constitutes an ethnic hierarchy in which the railway employees are the controllers and on top, while the Natives are underneath as subservient clients. This discriminatory structure is in place, sometimes subtle and at other times not so, at the railway station, the hotel, the restaurant and the police station. During my fieldwork, I began to pick up the clues, or unwritten rules of interaction, that served to structure discriminatory behaviour. My attempt to rent a room at the K.G. Hotel, for example, made it clear to me that I would only be allowed to stay there if I identified quite specifically with the local establishment, such as the Ministry of Natural Resources. When I was not sure about how the existing structure operated or about how my actions would be perceived by others, then I felt ambivalent about what my role should be. When I called on the police officer next door, for example, to help me get back into the house, I was conscious of the chance that others might see me visiting the officer.

My feeling of ambivalence stemmed partly from my need to please both parties. The Ojibwa people were an important, one could say crucial, part of my anthropological studies, and so I felt the need to stay on good terms with them. This could be facilitated, I thought, if I didn't identify overtly or too strongly with those at the top of the power structure, such as the police. On the other hand, I needed the assistance of railway people to find out about the trains, of the hotel owner for a place to stay, and of the police should I encounter any difficulty.

Such fieldwork problems as I was encountering in Armstrong are described by other ethnographers who have felt anxiety and ambivalence in their own field situations. The stress of fieldwork stems partly from the fieldworker's attempt to establish a rapport with strangers and partly from the alien milieu in which anthropologists are apt to find themselves. In a paper entitled "The Ethnologist as Stranger," for example, Nash writes that "in establishing rapport, and in attempting to acquire fairly complete data on the culture in a few months, the ethnologist encounters an extreme condition of strangership which lends a 'do or die' atmosphere to his expedition. For few other strangers is the adaptive problem so extreme, and for few does so much hinge on successful adaptation" (1963: 157).

We might call Nash's problem the "stress of involvement" in fieldwork. He suggests that anthropologists are likely to be more productive in their fieldwork when they can separate personal feelings from the pursuit of their academic goals. Personally, I found this separation difficult to achieve, mainly because I tended to identify with my Ojibwa informants, whom I regarded as my friends and confidants. The first time that I boarded the train for Collins, the conductor put me on the spot with the question, "Why in the hell would you want to go there?" He evidently saw the small Ojibwa communities along the rail-line as hellholes of fighting, incest and drunkenness. I saw his views as not only prejudicial but largely inaccurate. I nonetheless felt a certain amount of stress because of my involvement with him.

My experiences in Armstrong and elsewhere along the rail-line made me aware of the sometimes ambiguous and stressful roles to which anthropologists sometimes have to adjust. The intense involvement that fieldwork usually demands is apt to lead to a commitment that goes beyond just data collection. Peter Gutkind's fieldwork in East Africa is a good example of how the stress from such involvement can generate conflicts in the conduct of one's professional tasks. Gutkind's fieldwork was conducted in Lagos, Nigeria, among unemployed workers, who were always asking Gutkind to intercede for them with government officials in order to find them jobs. This situation was one that "put me under intense pressure to 'do something for them,' but this I was unable to do" (Gutkind 1969: 30). The unemployed Nigerians felt that the anthropologist could play a role in helping to alleviate their economic plight. There is often some confusion among the informants about what the fieldworker's role actually is, and they might see the fieldworker as one whose purpose is to aid them in some manner. Attempts to maintain a neutral stance may not always be tenable in fieldwork. Conducting an interview may involve the researcher indicating some degree of agreement or sympathy with a particular point of view. In my case in Armstrong, I felt some tension and conflict because of my perception that I was "caught" between respondents—the Ojibwa on one side and white railway employees on the other. It was precisely this kind of predicament that led Henry (1966) to argue that in certain cases, such as in her studies where interaction with an elite population was crucial to the successful outcome of her research, some degree of commitment or identification to the people studied on the part of the researcher is essential.

In fieldwork the anthropologist occupies a precarious role fraught with potential difficulties of identification, involvement, tension and even hostility. The fieldworker's political persuasions and personal temperament are added factors which complicate the fieldworker's role. When Malinowski made his comment about "that cold-blooded passion for sheer accuracy which the anthropologist can provide" (1970: 20), I wonder if he gave enough thought to the degree to which it is possible to separate one's personal life from the academic sides of research. Heggenhoughen (1992) argues for a theory of knowledge that propounds the interdependence of reason and emotion, and of objectivity and subjectivity, in the process of learning that is fieldwork.

Is it not all part of accepting the "reality," no matter how perceived, of what we find in our various fieldwork situations, rather than seeing in them what we would like or prefer? This, essentially, was the epistemological problem that David Stymeist (1975) faced in his study of a CNR town similar to Armstrong that he called "Crow Lake." Crow Lake is really a pseudonym for Sioux Lookout, a town of about five thousand people north of Dryden, not far from the Manitoba border. It is also a town that I visited on a fairly frequent basis, usually in the company of other Collins people, as we went for some entertainment or to buy groceries and other supplies.

My first impression of Sioux Lookout was that I knew the place because I knew Armstrong. What I mean to say is that my familiarity with the structured patterns of interaction in the railway town of Armstrong left me with certain expectations about Sioux Lookout. The main difference between the two towns is that Sioux Lookout is much larger than Armstrong, has more businesses, two hospitals—a so-called "Zone Hospital" for the sole use of Native people run by the Department of Indian Affairs (now no longer in operation) and a "public" one—and an Indian Affairs complex that administers a very large area of northwestern Ontario. It also has the usual northern institutions—a Ministry of Natural Resources base, a large (CNR) railway employed population and a fleet of fly-in tourist operators.

When I visited Sioux Lookout with Collins people, we stayed at the Sioux Hotel, and people were puzzled as to why a white man would want to stay in an "Indian hotel," as they called it. The structure of the Sioux Hotel was interesting. In the basement was the entertainment area. Bands were comprised of Metis and Native people who played raucous country-and-western-style music in a Cree-Ojibwa dialect. People in the audience were hooting and hollering all evening; apparently the songs were full of sexual and racial innuendo that was pretty much beyond my limited capacity to understand. After the bar closed, patrons were forced to go outside and back through the main entrance in order to get back into their rooms. Of course, once outside the hotel, they were deemed to be "in a public place" and were therefore subject to all manner of liquor related charges by the police.

In Stymeist's case, he knew little about the interactive patterns of the town, but like most new people he was struck by the natural beauty of the northern environment. At first he worked as a cab driver and then later as an ambulance operator for the Zone Hospital. Driving a cab and an ambulance was a good cover for his main job as an ethnographic fieldworker and allowed him the opportunity to witness much of the "behind the scenes" behaviour in the town. For example, when there was talk of disbanding the Zone Hospital and amalgamating it with the General, he was asked by one of the employees at the General Hospital: "If the hospitals join together, the women of our town would have to give birth to their children with Indians lying in the next bed. If you were going to have a baby, how would you feel if you found one of those long, black Indian hairs in the linen?" (1975: 93).

This is all part of the social reality with which First Nations residents must cope in northern Ontario. It is a reality that one is not necessarily apt to know much about through interviews or questionnaires but mainly through partici-pant-observation in such towns as Sioux Lookout and Armstrong. It takes a while for an outsider, who because of their own privilege are ignorant of racism and discrimination, to learn about the social and institutional context by which discriminatory patterns of behaviour become part of the enculturation process. After you have travelled along the CNR line and visited or lived in the small towns and villages along the way, you notice that disparaging comments are made about Native people by the white population all the time. It becomes so commonplace that you hardly even notice it after a while, if you are white.

The class system in many northern Ontario towns is very obvious. Occu-pying roles of ascendancy in this scheme are Indian Affairs administrators, senior positions on the railway, business and tourist operators, and police officers. First Nations people are situated lower down on the socio-economic scale; they usually work as guides in tourist operations or as seasonal labourers on the railway. The general theme here is one of domination by the ascendant groups through various control and boundary maintenance mechanisms. On the basis of Stymeist's fieldwork in Sioux Lookout, he chose to discard his initial theoretical focus on ethnicity and to adopt a viewpoint based on discrimination and prejudice. As he articulates his conclusion: "Prejudice and discrimination are important to the community, for whether or not the people of Crow Lake are fully aware of it, the town as a whole is heavily dependent upon the existence of a separate, unequal, and adjacent Native population" (1975: 93).

For many Canadians, who view their country in relatively benign terms, such a conclusion might be difficult to understand. "After all, we don't have a system of apartheid in Canada like South Africa had, do we?" they might say. This problem of perception, for many Canadians, has to do with a confusion over the official government policy of multiculturalism. At one level, it is an ideal promoted as a matter of official public policy in Canada. However, the reality of the actual behavioural patterns and the institutional structures in which people operate perpetuate unequal race relations.

My main point in the preceding discussion concerning places such as Sioux Lookout and Armstrong, and probably hundreds of other northern Canadian locales as well, is that the immense gap between how people perceive their society and the reality of actual behavioural practices is a topic that could be made a more explicit area of fieldwork in anthropology. For it is only through fieldwork, with its participatory and observational techniques conducted in the on-going flow of social life, that we gain glimpses of the structured patterns of behaviour that coalesce into the actual institutional bases of society. The fieldworker in situations involving ethnic and racial tension is apt to be forced to deal with considerable personal stress. Partly this emanates from a fractured sense of commitment over whether our fieldwork conducted to further theoretical knowledge in our discipline or to facilitate in some way practical solutions to the sorts of human problems we encounter. Stress also comes from feelings of social injustice as the fieldworker sees people (usually the ones regarded as our friends and informants) treated in a prejudicial and discriminatory manner. There is usually not very much that one can do about such situations during the course of one's fieldwork, and this sense of impotence can lead to some personal trauma as well.

It is prudent I believe to remember that there were originally concrete reasons why one was conducting the fieldwork in the first place and that a well-defined, focused study should be at the forefront of one's motivations. If not, then the study is apt to have a disintegrating research agenda because of the desire on the part of fieldworkers to adopt a more practical or problem-solving approach.

The Armstrong Experience

In one sense the town of Armstrong was part of my "community" of study. I had to be in Armstrong on a fairly frequent basis. In order to get to Collins I invariably had to pass through Armstrong. There was the odd time that I hired a bush plane to make the trip, but most of the time this journey meant taking the CNR passenger train. There were many occasions when the regular arrival time was late at night, or when the train was delayed for some reason, which meant spending many hours or even days hanging around the town. I also went to Armstrong frequently to buy groceries or other supplies at the Hudson's Bay store or to check on a vehicle that I usually had stashed away in the town somewhere.

Armstrong was also part of this community of study because of the frequent contacts that Collins people themselves maintained there. Visiting among relatives in the two towns was a common pastime. In a sense, places such as Collins, Armstrong and the other nearby rail-line villages could be considered one large community of interaction. This was because they share a common history of emergence along the railway tracks, their communities of origin (such as Fort Hope or the reserves around Lake Nipigon) are mostly the same, and most people have many close relatives in these other villages.

In terms of my fieldwork experience I never saw my studies in Collins in terms of a distinct, isolated social organization. In fact, I realized that if I wanted to find out what was going on in Collins, it was necessary for me to know a lot about the historical development, social organization, interaction patterns and so on in the neighbouring communities as well. My viewpoint, in social, economic and political terms was at the regional, rather than local, level.

This regional perspective, however, tended to cause some problems for my fieldwork. While in Armstrong, for example, I always felt an inner tension. I was never too comfortable being there. When I thought about it, this feeling of tension originated from a sensation of ambivalence towards the town and its people. Tension also stemmed to some degree from my own personal insecurities about being there in the first place. I felt uncomfortable about dealing with Armstrong's white-dominated power structure—the hotel operator, police, CNR personnel and the like. In Collins, the community social organization did not have this heavy "overlay" of Euro-Canadian authority figures. Maybe my discomfort had to do with my too idyllic sense of what fieldwork in anthropology should be—one traditionally studies in a fairly homogeneous community. There seemed to be too much tension in Armstrong, "ethnic" or otherwise, that made me feel uncomfortable. In retrospect, this ambivalence and insecurity was probably caused by my inability to fully accept the social reality as it actually existed in Armstrong. Instead, I saw the social order in Armstrong in pathological terms, as a social problem that should be rectified in some way. I saw life in Collins, in contrast, as one of cooperation and harmony, even though there were probably just as many problems there as in Armstrong.

It is useful for ethnographers to examine, after the fact, the reasons why we view situations, events and people the way we do. At one time all I had was a raw, gut feeling that Collins felt more like home to me, while Armstrong for whatever reason was not a comfortable place for me to be in. When I thought about it further, I had certain feelings concerning social justice and the like which placed Armstrong, in terms of my viewpoint, in an unfavourable light. I realize now that acceptance of what we find in the field, even if such situations run contrary to our own personal beliefs, is the only sound methodological approach to whatever problem we happen to be working on. If we think a situation in the field is aberrant, imbued with injustice or otherwise inherently wrong, then the main philosophical underpinning of anthropology having to do with the concept of cultural relativism will work to our disadvantage. It does not mean as social scientists that we have to like what we find in the field. It just means that we accept our findings in as objective a manner as our intellectual capabilities will permit.

Chapter Five

Up at Whitewater Lake

It was only as the hum of the motor faded into the snow-heavy clouds
that I fully realized where I was. Realization came in the form of a
peculiar sense not of loneliness but of separateness, of having no
context for my existence... no bond of language, of understanding, or
of shared experience linked me with the silent Eskimo behind me. —
Jean Briggs (1970: 23)

Armstrong and Whitewater Lake, as far as my fieldwork in northern Ontario
was concerned, were similar in several important facets. Both locales involved
research outside of the familiar confines of the Collins community which,
because of their dissimilarity to Collins, forced me to develop new avenues of
investigation, to overcome new and different sorts of problems, and to relate the
research issues that I found in Collins to a much wider sphere of intellectual
activity. On the other hand, research in these outside areas involved quite
different conditions of fieldwork.

Armstrong has a more urban setting, with automobiles, streets, restaurants
and hotels. It also has a more diversified or multi-faceted social organization
than Collins, with its over-lay of Euro-Canadian authority figures. By contrast,
the Whitewater Lake camp was back in the bush and more isolated than either
Collins or Armstrong. At Whitewater, the characteristics of the social organization were pretty much defined by the work activities necessitated by the
construction of the tourist lodge. The hierarchy was one of construction bosses,
foremen, skilled workers (electricians, carpenters, plumbers, etc.) and labourers. The camp was also composed of the wives and children of the workers, who
had set up about a dozen campsites of varying sizes in the vicinity of the
construction site. These families lived in tents and engaged in hunting and
fishing to meet their subsistence needs. In this regard, the Whitewater social
organization had a much more "traditional" appearance than either Collins or
Armstrong. But appearances can be deceiving; there was no reason to assume
that, because of similarities in the physical set-up to traditional Native bush
camps, there was any similarity to the traditional social make-up of such camps.

In fact, one of the research areas I began to work on at Whitewater Lake
was the social composition of the bush camps and how they compared with
Ojibwa residential groups in the past, as described by previous ethnographers,
for example, an Ojibwa community in the 1950s (Robert Dunning 1959). My
research strategy was to document the characteristics of Whitewater social

organization in terms of kinship ties and the step-by-step evolution of the camps. My main goal was to determine to what extent the wage economy at Whitewater was a determining factor in group composition and compare that to the extent to which economic factors in previous decades, such as those existing in the fur-trade period of the 1950s and before, were significant factors in group composition.

New research perspectives were necessitated by the different settings of Armstrong and Whitewater Lake, which forced me to be intellectually creative in ways distinct from those utilized in Collins. The research problems that presented themselves to me were different in each of these three separate settings; yet they all had to be tied together at a higher level of abstraction. I related the problems in the different settings to issues relating to social organization, economic pursuits and leadership characteristics. In a curious sort of way, I was intrigued by the Collins-Armstrong-Whitewater triad. For Collins people, the activities at Whitewater Lake were seen as a return to a fondly remembered past of bush life, while the view of Armstrong was that of a disconcerting future of ethnic strife and tension.

I sensed that much of the appeal for Collins people of life at Whitewater Lake was that it was an ideal amalgamation of the traditional and modern worlds. At Whitewater, people could make a decent living from the wage economy while at the same time enjoy the outdoor life of fishing, campfires and fresh air. They were also optimistic about the future, in which they could continue their life in the bush, engaged in economic activities that they liked doing and had some measure of control over. As a fieldworker, I participated in this dream to some extent as I shared in the people's vision of a better future.

I was intrigued, also, by another facet of research at Whitewater Lake— having to do with the activities of a long-term resident named Wendel Beckwith. Wendel was an eccentric hermit who had his own research agenda, involving geological and cosmological measurements, but he also had a very good rapport with the Ojibwa people in the area. He also played an important role in the tourist lodge construction because of his innovative designs that were incorporated into the architectural plans for the various buildings.

Whitewater Lake

Whitewater Lake is situated about three hundred and fifty kilometres north of Thunder Bay. In the fur trading era, it was part of an important chain of lakes and rivers which comprised, via the Ogoki and Albany rivers, a major transportation route linking the interior of northern Ontario with the Hudson's Bay Company posts on James Bay. Today, while still in a remote and relatively inaccessible region, it is known more as an attraction for adventurous canoeists and sports fishers than for its productivity in beaver pelts. It was because of the relatively pristine environment and abundance of pickerel that the residents of

Collins decided to built a tourist lodge on Whitewater Lake, hoping to establish a tourist industry that would form the basis of a reliable local economy.

I had the good fortune of arriving in Collins when the tourist lodge project was still in the planning stages, so there was an opportunity for me to study various aspects of the construction process from its initial inception to eventual completion. The facets of the construction that interested me concerned the Collins' leadership group, the Ogoki River Guides (ORG), and its negotiations with government officials over the funding for the lodge (it eventually cost over a million dollars to build). Also of interest were the economic aspects of construction, such as the structure of work crews and their duties, as well as the social organization of family life in and around the lodge site.

My fieldwork at Whitewater Lake was somewhat subsidiary to my main ethnographic interest in the village of Collins, but I did spend the better part of one summer living in the base camp of the construction site. In addition, I spent time in the area with other people, such as Ojibwa families working as fishing guides for other tourist operators, and Wendel Beckwith, who lived on the other side of Whitewater Lake on Best Island.

This chapter describes these experiences at Whitewater Lake, while showing how I studied the various facets of the camp that interested me at the time. I begin here with my first visit up to Whitewater by snowmobile to meet Wendel Beckwith on a extremely cold winter day in January.

Wendel, the "White Hermit"

The rumble of a snow machine outside my cabin door was louder than usual, and I looked out to see Donald beckoning me to come and see his new toy. The machine was called an "Elite," which I took to represent to him his pre-eminent social position in the community. It was like no snow machine that I had ever seen before. The engine was in the back, which I was to discover later didn't do much for keeping us warm. Also, the passenger and driver sat side by side in the front like in a car rather than like on a motorcycle.

"Let's go for a drive," he shouted over the noise of the machine.

I had envisioned a short trip around the village, but he said that we would be going farther so I should pile on more clothes. Little did I know that over the next two days we would travel about two hundred kilometres through the bush. Donald had in mind a visit up to Whitewater Lake to test out his new machine and to see how his friend, the white hermit Wendel Beckwith, was doing.

All through the day we skimmed across long stretches of open ice at high rates of speed. Occasionally, we made short detours over the portage trail in the bush, but what I remember most was the constant blast of frigid air in my face, the high pitched whine of the machine, and the fact that we received no heat from the engine because of the strange configuration of the motor. Finally, at about five o'clock in the evening, we approached a small trapper's cabin, and cheering children ran out to great us. My right leg had been sticking out over the edge of the machine for most of the trip, and when I tried to step out, it sort of locked, causing me to fall face-first into the snow. I was embarrassed and felt stiff and clumsy. Inside the cabin we had a chance to get warm for a bit, and were served some tea and bannock. I remember that the trapper was a large, barrel-chested man. He took a loaf of bannock about ten inches around, sliced it in two with his hunting knife and laid inside of it two pieces of fried pickerel. He then prepared to eat this hefty sandwich with relish, but his wife began to admonish him, presumably because she thought he was over-eating in front of their guests.

Anyway, we couldn't stay long. Donald explained that we had to try to get over to Best Island on the other side of the lake before it got too dark. So off we went again for a short, ten-mile jaunt to visit the hermit Wendel. The moon was out by the time we got there. I was amazed to find two beautifully crafted log cabins, with a faint light glowing in one of them. Wendel came out to greet us. He was a thin man, with a crackly sort of laugh, and long hair held back by a headband. Wendel explained that his cabin was very cold because he was in the middle of conducting an experiment on cold weather adaptation, but he would put a fire in the stove so we could warm up.

I noticed that his cabin was filled with esoteric odds and ends and that there were rows of notebooks on the upper shelves. Wendel entertained us with his stories throughout the evening and I must admit that he is one of the most interesting, yet inscrutable, characters I have ever met. We ate a little canned corn and fried potatoes. I relaxed and looked around. Against one wall was a couch with a strange crank and pulley apparatus hooked up to it. He explained that this was his bed and that it was divided in the middle so that it would fold up out of the way. Another interesting apparatus was a dumb waiter of sorts that he had carved out of the rock and sand below the cabin which served as a cold storage compartment.

Wendel's story was that he was a former employee of an engineering firm in Milwaukee and that the owner of the firm, his benefactor, had subsidized his trip into northern Ontario. This particular location, eighty kilometres north of Armstrong, because of its longitude and latitude, had significant geological and cosmologic properties, Wendel explained. He never got around to relating in any detail what these properties were except to make reference to similarities to the Greenwich time zone in England. Most of our conversation was about obscure or enigmatic scientific ideas. Wendel had been in this area nearly ten years by this time. Like many recluses, he saw himself as a victim of the establishment, which regarded his work as incomprehensible. He now cared little for what members of the scientific establishment thought. He had his work to do and was content in carrying it out as he saw fit, unencumbered by the outside world.

The various devices and apparatuses in and around his cabins were most intriguing. Outside the front door was a slice of a log about an inch thick by a foot across. This piece of wood had a triangular shaped crack in it, with a wire extending out from the middle to which was attached a nail. The face of the log had various makings on it, inscribed to indicate certain measurements. Wendel explained that this device was his "weather-humidity gauge"—the gap in the wood would fluctuate in and out as the humidity changed, allowing him to make relatively accurate measurements of changing atmospheric conditions.

Wendel also claimed to be the co-inventer of the ballpoint pen, and he held a certain bitterness towards some unscrupulous patent experts who, he claimed, had robbed him of this recognition. He told us a story of his younger days, when he came across a pile of old auto parts of Model T vintage. He proceeded over the ensuing few days to build a vehicle from this assemblage and then undertook to traverse the Western United States in it. This "car" however had no brakes, and he eventually wrecked it at the bottom of a steep hill.

After all these stories, it was getting late and time for bed. I was given a small cot set against the far wall in an elevated section of the cabin. There would be no heat in the stove, he explained, but there was a large pile of blankets that we could use. I prepared for the worse, got on my parka and extra clothes, but was unable to keep in much heat. I piled up one blanket on top of another, but the added weight just seemed to squeeze out my body heat. To make matters worse, Wendel had a small, short-haired dog who kept whining and trying to burrow into my blankets, despite the numerous times I swatted it off. It was a cold, sleepless night.

By morning, I was still groggy and extremely stiff, especially in the legs, from sleeping with them all cramped up. It took me a while to get moving. Wendel, on the other hand, had been up for some time and had a cheery demeanour. After breakfast, he showed me various coloured drawings that he was working on, plans for yet another cabin. This one would be built into the side of a sandy hill on the other side of the island, to take advantage of the southern exposure. The back of the structure was to have a long chute, like loading a magazine, which would be filled with logs so he would have a continuous feed of wood into his fireplace. With skylights and other innovations, this looked like it could be an interesting model for houses in the northern environment. His ideas kept bubbling up as if they had been suppressed all winter because of lack of conversation.

Before we left, I asked Wendel a question, something that I had been thinking about for many years. It had to do with a Viking sword that had been found in the bush by a prospector in the 1940s near the town of Beardmore, on the west shore of Lake Nipigon. As the story goes, there had been quite an excitement concerning this find in the scientific community, and apparently, for many years, the sword had even been displayed in a case in the main entrance to the Royal Ontario Museum in Toronto. There had never been other Viking finds in the area before, and people were at a loss to explain how or why the Vikings could ever have gotten up into this northern bush. Eventually, the conclusion of the archaeologists was that the sword, while genuine, had been planted near Beardmore for unknown reasons. It was removed from its display case in the 1950s and buried in the catacombs of the Museum's basement holdings.

I was surprised that Wendel did not take much time in formulating a theory. It crossed my mind that this was just the sort of thing that he had been thinking about for some time as well and, in fact, was part of the reason he was studying in this part of the world. As he related:

"The Vikings were great explorers and probably far better than history has given them credit for." Wendel stopped, drew in a long breath while he pulled strands of hair behind one ear and continued. "They not only went to Greenland and Newfoundland, but I would venture to say that they could not resist going down the St. Lawrence. It would be quite a task, but they would be capable of sailing through the Great Lakes, dismantling and hauling their ships over portages where necessary. Eventually they would find their way into Lake Superior, probably with thoughts of going home via a northern route into Hudson's Bay." At this point he paused and held his hand out, thumb up in the air, and moved it back and forth as if operating a rudder. "You know," he continued, "the secret of the Viking explorations was their ballast system. The boats were weighted down to keep them erect in the water, and the ballast had a very high iron content, possibly composed of meteoric iron, which is relatively pure and found in abundance in the arctic regions."

I glanced over at Donald, who furrowed up his brow, as if he had difficulty following the convolutions of Wendel's anecdote. It was typical of Wendel's mode of reasoning that there were enough scientific facts involved that you were persuaded to accept the general lines of his argument, but there were leaps of logic, sometimes quite fantastic, that stretched your credulity, no matter how sympathetic you were to his esoteric genius.

What followed was the crux of his explanation about Viking voyages. "The iron-laden ballast in the Viking ships was the secret to their navigational success," Wendel explained. " On a calm day, with the ship sitting in motionless water, it would be drawn around into a north-south alignment, because the iron ballast acted as a sort of compass needle. The Vikings didn't need any sophisticated navigational aides because their ships had a built-in homing rod."

I became much more sceptical at this point but allowed Wendel to continue with what he saw as the proof of his theory. "Let's get out a glass and fill it to the top with water," he motioned in imaginary fashion as if pouring from a picture. "Now carefully pour in just a bit more water until there is a bulge of liquid on top of the glass. Now, very delicately, slide a pin or needle onto the top surface of this bulge in the water. What do you think will happen? This piece of steel, heavier than water, will not sink. It is held afloat by the surface tension of the water extruding over top of the vessel."

Wendel held out his hand again, duplicating the back and forth rudder motion. He then adopted a serious gaze, "And what else do you think will happen to the needle? You will notice that it begins to revolve around until it stops in a north-south alignment, drawn by the magnetic north pole. You can check it out with a compass, to verify it."

I interjected, "Wendel, I can understand about the Viking ships' ability to find their way north, even though I would have to see a demonstration of this in actual practice to believe it, but what does this all have to do with the Beardmore sword?"

"Well don't you see?" he said, pointing in the air, as if the point was obvious. "Everyone in North America would have known that the way you go from Lake Superior to James Bay is up the Nipigon River to Lake Nipigon. From the north end of Nipigon there is a series of long lakes—Caribou, Smooth Rock and Whitewater—right past my front door in fact. From here it is easy sailing into the Ogoki and Albany river system into James Bay. The fur traders always went this way, and so did the Indians for thousands of years. This travel route would have been the most obvious message that the Indians would have had for the Vikings, but there must have been translation problems. Beardmore is reached through the north-west portion of Lake Nipigon, and the entrance configuration of a large bay is similar to that leading up to the Ogoki. But in the Beardmore case, the river system just leads into a series of small lakes, rivers and eventually swamp. The Vikings, without their ballast aligner, would have been hopelessly lost in the bush, and like the Franklin expedition, would have floundered around in this vast territory to the last man."

I was stunned. Wendel's explanation was absolutely brilliant, especially since it was more-or-less off the cuff. Of course there was much that was left unexplained, such as why a sword (and possibly a shield) were the only artifacts found from a large contingent of men. Beardmore during the 1940s had three of the largest gold producing mines in the world, and prospectors would have scoured practically every inch of this region. Still, maybe the sword was traded to a local Ojibwa, who subsequently discarded it, with the Viking crew falling through the ice of a northern lake and thereby sealing all evidence of their existence. For quite some time I mulled over the various parts of Wendel's explanation and wondered what it would be like to spend some time in his head, thinking his thoughts.

Wendel liked his solitude, to do his studies and be left alone, although he would extend hospitality to those he regarded as friendly. The people from the immigration authority or the Ministry of Natural Resources did not fall into this category, and there are stories of him pushing their float planes away from his dock with a pole. Eventually, though, Wendel became concerned about what would happen to his place. He wanted it preserved in some way from those who would loot it and strip it clean after he was gone. One day, a planeload of government officials arrived to discuss what would be done with his place in the event that he wasn't able to look after it. Wendel wanted his Ojibwa friends, the people who had traplines in the area, to be the custodians. The government people disagreed, and a shouting match apparently ensued. As the story goes, Wendel left, to clear his head and take a walk down to the dock where he had spent so many hours looking out over the primordial beauty of Whitewater Lake. Some time later they found him stretched out at the end of the wharf, dead of an apparent heart attack. Wendel was a quiet, kind-hearted man, almost saintly, who couldn't find a place in the crude civilization of which he was a part.

Back to Whitewater

A trip by float plane over the northern bush country is both exciting and dull—a strange mixture of semi-panic and sleepiness. The roar of the plane's motor is exciting enough, as if it were straining far beyond its capacity. At any moment you expect to hear a sudden "thwop, thwop" sound as the propeller disengages and then the inevitable dive bomb to the crash landing below. There is so little distance between the plane and the tops of the spruce trees that the flying experience is more one of skimming an overgrown lawn than it is of actually being airborne. The flight is also dull because of the relatively monotonous terrain with its patches of blue and green. There is little topological relief to the country of the coniferous forest since it was not that long ago, in geological terms, that the glaciers scoured the land flat and left their melted pools for lakes and rivers.

As I glanced out the window my thoughts turned to the snowmobile trip up to Wendel's place the previous winter. All those blue patches had been frozen over then and how desolate it would have looked from this far up in the air. I also remember Wendel showing us drawings he was working on for a tourist lodge at Whitewater Lake. There would be a massive tee-pee style structure in the centre of the grounds. He envisioned that the outside skin for this structure would be of moose hides sewn together with waterproof stitching, like the type the Inuit used on their sealskin boots. Wendel was also working on his own version of "crazy glue" to help hold it all together, made from a concoction of sturgeon and goose eggs, if I remember correctly. I do remember that he had used this glue to secure the fletchings on some hunting arrows he had made. He took me outside to demonstrate how they worked. The bow was rather flimsy and the arrows were not particularly straight, so their flight took a weird, spiral path. The feathers stayed on though, and in his mind that was sufficient to prove the point he was making.

The leaders in Collins who were responsible for designing the tourist lodge project thought quite highly of Wendel and his designs. They worked out a modified plan which abandoned the moose hide idea in favour of cedar shingles, and so Wendel got to work on designing a chopping device so that the shakes could be made right at the site rather than imported from British Columbia or some other distant place. When it came down to making simple machinery, Wendel was the master of efficiency.

Wendel produced other designs that were both practical and aesthetically pleasing. Take, for example, his idea for the flooring of the guest cabins that would surround the main lodge. First, a thick layer of beach sand was laid down.

The actual floor was made by cutting blocks of wood into hexagonal shapes (using his shingle chopping device) so that they all fit together like the cells of a beehive. Caulking was applied to the outer edges of the blocks, then the whole floor was sanded smooth and finished with a layer of varnish. The cabins themselves were also hexagonal in shape, so that each individual room resembled a slice of pie. The supports for each of these rooms were fitted into a central fireplace, which had one chimney or flue but an opening for each room. Like most of Wendel's ideas, these were economical, practical and showed a marvellous, if somewhat eccentric, engineering insight, modeled on the natural world. He might have thought that bees had a million years to work out their design, so why not use it?

The plane's motor slowed down, and my mind snapped back to the reality of our plane circling around the bay at the end of Whitewater Lake. The construction site was visible below, but it was only a cleared patch of ground—Wendel's designs had not become reality yet. I also noticed that it was starting to become dark, and the pilot was anxious to unload his cargo and get airborne again without delay. He motioned to the other side of the bay, as he twirled a device to lower the rear flaps. "That's where all the people are camped," he said. "Do you see the smoke coming up through the trees? Somebody will see our plane land and come over to get you by boat—you can't walk over there." I was amazed at how quickly he was able to land and then jump back into the air again.

From the clearing, I watched as the roar of the plane's motor became an ever quieter drone and the plane disappeared into the sunset. There didn't seem to be much here—a partially constructed shed, a few digging tools scattered about, a large stack of logs and that was about it. But I soon realized that there were clouds of mosquitoes and blackflies coming out of the bush in waves. Was I the only warm blooded creature left in the universe? I had to think quickly or I would be eaten alive. The bugs were already crawling up my sleeves and into my hair, and I was starting to look like I was covered with fur. There was also no sign of any rescue by boat, as the pilot had promised.

My first thought was, "What would be the best way to attract the campers on the opposite shore and get rid of the bugs at the same time? Of course," I thought, " a fire would do the trick." If they thought that their construction site was about to burn up, they would surely rush over. So I got busy scraping together some dry leaves and twigs into a pile. Once this little blaze was going at a good clip, I smothered it with a pile of green leaves. I then stepped into the middle of this inferno, caring little for my safety at this point as long as I wasn't getting bitten any more. A thick column of white smoke funnelled up around me in a comforting aroma of cedar, pine needles and birch leaves. It didn't take long for the alarm to be sounded at the base camp, and I could hear the commotion across the bay as the aluminum boats banged against the rocks and the outboard motors roared into action.

Moss Bag Retreat

My rescue party consisted of a single boat driven by a man I recognized as Tommy W., but I didn't think he was part of the construction crew. When he recognized me, Tommy started into an involved explanation about how he volunteered to see what the smoke was about because he had to pick something up here anyway. He then proceeded to convince me in the most earnest fashion to accompany him to the far side of the lake, where his family was camped. Tommy was working for a tourist operator there, as part of a fly-in operation linking Whitewater and the Ogoki River. Anyway, he explained, his wife and children were coming back to this base camp the following afternoon and I could return with them if I wished. Tommy took out his Winchester rifle and steadied it at the stern of the boat. I thought that this action was a preparation in the event that he should spot a moose swimming across the lake. We sped off into the semi-darkness, leaving all those nasty mosquitoes behind in a stationary cloud.

In no time at all, we were virtually in complete darkness, as there was not much of a moon out. The starlight glistened off the waves, the motor hummed along at a steady roar, and I marvelled at how Tommy could find his way through this channel, around this island and so on, mile after mile in the nondescript terrain that was hardly visible by now.

It took about two hours for our trip, the motor slowed its pace and my hearing started to return. I noticed a long section of land jutting into the lake with what appeared to be several white canvas tents pitched near the end of this peninsula. The other thing I noticed was the rather eerie sight of long strands of moss blowing in the wind, like so many beards of decapitated men. It puzzled me what this was all about. Tommy paid no attention to this strange sight, as he hurried to haul the boat up on shore. "Well, here we are, make yourself at home," he said with a snicker.

There was also the oddest sight, to my mind at least, of an electric wringer washing machine sitting out here in the middle of nowhere. It was evidently hooked up to a small generator and was probably brought in by plane, but it was no doubt of immense practical help to the women of the camp. The tents housed several families and were set up on plywood platforms. The wind blew incessantly, the sides of the tents flapped loudly most of the time, and I wondered if I would get used to the noise. Then I remembered the mosquitoes and thought no more about the reason why we were camped on this windy finger of land.

Tommy pulled back the opening flap, and we crawled into a dimly lit area. His wife, named Otsie in Ojibwa, but Elizabeth in English, hardly looked up. She was busy attending to a baby that was stretched out on its back, and then I realized what the dried moss was for—it was used as a lining or diaper for the child, whose bottom was then wrapped in a sort of "bag" as they called it. The baby was then stuffed inside the opening of a cradle board, or *tikenahgen*, which had several laces up in front.

There seemed to be some nervousness about me watching this operation, but it wasn't long before we were all asleep, sprawled out across the floor. First thing in the morning I heard the crackling fire outside and smelled bacon frying. In short order, there was an elaborate breakfast set out for me. I appreciated the effort although I didn't feel that hungry. It struck me that this was the sort of shore lunch that the tourists would eat before their fishing trip, and, as a white man, maybe Otsie thought that this was what we expected to eat every morning.

Before long we were back in the boat skipping across the water, away from my "moss bag retreat." Otsie was as adept as her husband at skirting around the islands and maneuvering through the channels. Even though it was daylight, I felt just as confused about the terrain as I had the night before. Heaven forbid, I thought, if I ever became lost out here.

The Whitewater Base Camp

It didn't seem to take as long returning as it had the night before. Otsie skillfully guided the boat up to the rocks near the base camp. I grabbed my old green pack and skipped out, uttering a short "Thanks," as I left. That was all we had ever said to one another.

Here, there were about eight or ten white canvas tents, most of which were pitched on platforms in a manner similar to Tommy's place. There were also more elaborate designs, as some tents were erected over a frame of spruce poles with walls four or five feet tall. A small kitchen area was crowded into the central area of the camp, and I was told that there were quite a few other families camped out along the shore and on the island across from the bay. This base camp was mainly for the single men, who shared sleeping space, two or three men to a tent.

I had made arrangements to stay with a young engineering student from New Zealand whose brother's firm was employed to coordinate the building of the tourist lodge. He was an amiable chap and made room in the tent for my sleeping bag. The odd reminiscence that I have of this first encounter was his comment that the mosquitoes had no effect on him. Only later did I learn that he was taking pills of some sort that reduced the effects of the bugs' bites.

The country about the camp was pristine. There was hardly any underbrush, and the ground was covered with a thick layer of sphagnum moss. There were also various types of mushrooms, large and small, growing in the moss, and I made a mental note to buy a book on mushrooms on my next trip out. The moss, though, held in a lot of moisture which made walking a soggy venture.

There were numerous airplanes arriving throughout the day, and I was busy recording the comings and goings of the people involved. I was particularly interested in the manner in which a camp was forming on an island site across the bay from the base camp. It started off occupied by two sisters (Montreal's daughters) and their husbands and children. Then the extended family of one of the husbands arrived (his mother, single brother, and two sisters). And later, one of these sisters' husbands landed with his own parents. I began to make kinship diagrams of these various relationships, and found an intricate pattern of family ties involved. The emerging formation of this camp seemed to me to be an opportunity to develop an hypothesis about the formation of bush-oriented residential groups under conditions of a wage-work economy.

Analyzing Field Data

My field notes are filled with comments about the various kinship relationships and what their possible significance could be. The people themselves seemed to feel that they just moved where "they felt like it," and I was disappointed with the lack of a more "structuralist" orientation to their explanations. Other books on the social structure of the northern Ojibwa (Dunning 1959 and Rogers 1962, for example) appear to have consistent patterns involved in the explanations of community life, and yet here I struggled with many contradictions and unresolved sociological problems. As it turned out, there was an important lesson for me here, and that is to try and accept the field data as it is, as you properly recorded it. It is the differences that one finds from the work of previous ethnographers, rather than the similarities, that are most important and are most apt to lead to new insights.

These new insights in my case had to do with the way people employed the pre-existing social relationships back in their home community of Collins in flexible patterns to adapt to the conditions of the wage-work setting at Whitewater Lake. Here from my field notes is an example of the way I began to work out these issues:

Step 1: Describe the Relationships

> August 27th
> Tommy Quissis returned [to Whitewater Lake] this morning from Collins with his wife Helen and their three girls. They will set up camp beside the Kwandibens as Helma, Helen's sister, is married to Victor K. The evolution of the Kwandibens' camp began with Victor, his wife Helma and widowed mother Charlotte. Victor's brother Morris, a single man, joined them shortly after from the base camp. Next, the brother's sister, Harriette and her husband Adam Yellowhead set up camp. The camp is further augmented by Harriette's sister, Helen Wynn, and her husband Steve. Steve's parents, Sinclair and Daisy Wynn, then move close by. The camp is completed when Adam's brother, Elijah, a single man from the base camp, moved in with the group. Sinclair's wife Daisy is a sister to Adam and Elijha Yellowhead.

The following day I attempted a preliminary analysis of the relationships in this camp, trying to account for their formation in light of various historical, cultural and economic conditions.

Step 2: Account for the Patterns

> August 28th
> An analysis of the structure of this co-residential group demonstrates
> the significance of the solidarity of brothers in the alignment of
> residence patterns. There is also operative a solidarity of sisters,
> provided their husbands have no close male kinsmen in the area. This
> is indicated by Tommy Q.'s and Adam Y.'s decision to join the
> Kwandibens group even though Tommy has a brother and father in the
> area— but both of whom are widowed and live in the base camp—and
> even though Adam's sister lives close by. However Adam's single
> brother Elijah moved into the Wynn [section of the] camp. The
> solidarity of male kinsmen is further indicated by Steve W.'s decision
> to take up residence in his father's part of the camp, rather than close
> by to his wife's family, ie., the Kwandibens.

An attempt was then made to push this preliminary analysis into a wider sphere
of discussion by way of outlining an hypothesis to account for the formation of
this particular camp on the basis of more general historical factors.

Step 3: Develop an Hypothesis

> Log cabins have a permanency associated with them that inhibits the
> formation and re-organization of co-residential groups. Whitewater
> camp grounds provide an experimental setting for incipient co-
> residential group formation. There is a paucity of material in the
> literature on the evolution of these groups. Also, the significance of
> certain relationships, such as a number of dominant brothers as the
> core of the co-residential group, tends to be assumed beforehand.
> One may argue that changes in the structure of co-residential
> groups have resulted from acculturation and an entry into the Euro-
> Canadian wage economy. In the fur trade economy a group of brothers
> who were good hunters and trappers contributed the most to the
> group. It is assumed that the evolution of these groups began with a
> group of brothers about whom concentric rings of relatives through
> marriage become attached to these patrilateral kinsmen. The wage
> economy allows for less dependence upon hunting and fishing for
> survival as more food can be store-bought than is possible on a trapper's
> income.
> Hypothesis: The evolution of residential groups in the context of
> a wage-work economic system tend to develop on an ad hoc basis,
> depending upon pre-existing relationships with individuals already
> settled into the work camp.

This, then, is the general pattern of analysis by which I proceeded. First, there was a documentation of particular cases as accurately as possible. Two modes of analysis then took place: first, examining the various inter-relationships and general patterns of the specific details involved in the internal patterns of the cases; then, second, a more wide-ranging thinking about what these specific instances could possibly mean in the larger context of the literature on Ojibwa sociology and cultural practices.

From my fieldwork experiences at Whitewater Lake, I learned that it is this documentation of specific details that was the most important aspect of my study. It provided the concrete foundation that I could return to over and over again for subsequent re-analysis and interpretation. The other modes of analysis were also important but for different reasons. The analysis made in the field serves more to provide an orientation for what one is doing than to lay out in any specific way the wording of the analysis that will eventually take place at the write-up stage. What the preliminary analysis does is force you to think about general patterns and arguments while actually living in the field, which in turn, has an effect on what field material you are apt to collect. The analysis will probably change later, sometimes in a major way, but this has the side benefit of allowing you to see the way your thinking changed over the course of the fieldwork, as well as the way ideas get started and how they relate to the issues you think are important during the very preliminary stages of data collection.

Daily Camp Life

Incidents occurred from time to time that were not directly related to my primary research theme but which I felt should be recorded for future reference. This somewhat humorous incident that took place concerning an island campsite is one example. About six o'clock one morning, there was quite a commotion going on over at this camp. We were startled at this early hour by rifle shots and women yelling, which we over at the base camp took to be the outbreak of some violent incident. In actual fact, a moose had swum over to the island and become entangled in the guy ropes which held up the tents. While most of the people were still sleeping, the moose up-rooted the tents and began to drag them over the occupants and through the still smoldering coals of the cooking fires. Several men woke in a daze and, dimly seeing the outline of the moose in the morning haze and lake mist, took "pot-shots" in its direction. The moose managed to untangle itself and soon disappeared, leaving behind a considerable state of confusion. Imagine having to start your day with all your belongings strewn about the campsite, most of them having been dragged across the damp ground and through black charcoal. At least there was a lot for everyone to laugh about that morning.

The kitchen at the base camp was worked by a woman in her fifties and a younger assistant. The breakfast usually consisted of fried eggs and toast.

Supplies of sliced meat and bread were then laid out so that the men could make sandwiches for their mid-day meal. Food for supper often consisted of fish, such as pickerel, sturgeon and pike, caught at Whitewater Lake. Sometimes the fish was filleted and fried, but often it was made into a soup with potatoes and onions. Hunks of fish were cut into squares about an inch wide, and almost all of the fish was included, even the head. The cheeks, especially of lake trout, are considered a delicacy. Fried bannock, a heavy bread made with flour, salt and baking powder was also served at just about every meal. I found it a bit strange scooping up pieces of fish from the large cook pot with these fish heads bobbing up and down, staring back at me.

My recollection is that while I enjoyed the fish, after about two weeks of eating at the base camp, my stomach began to rebel at all the fried food. I woke up in the middle of the night with this intense burning sensation and immediately ran down to the lake and drank large quantities of water. This did little to alleviate my distress, so I went over to the kitchen where I found an open case of Carnation evaporated milk. I reasoned that the milk would help to counteract the acidity and proceeded to gulp down two or three cans of this sweet liquid. The milk itself was almost enough to make me sick, but it did ease the pain enough for me to go back to sleep.

Even though it was only near the end of August, the weather had gotten surprisingly cold. I had actually started to wear my winter parka, something I learned to carry with me all year round, because even on the hottest summer days, as a trip across one of the larger lakes could be a very cold experience, especially if the wind was blowing. I noticed that people were beginning to construct small, porch-like structures in front of their tents and had hooked up woodstoves, or "tin heaters" in these entrance ways. I was sure it was going to snow.

After several days into this cold spell, we were startled to hear a loud bang, which sounded like an explosion, outside the camp. It was barely daylight, but everyone ran out to the edge of the lake and tried to get a glimpse of what was going on. It was a confusing sight because of the mist rising off the warm water into the cold air. There was a pile of debris floating in the middle of the bay, about mid-way between the base camp and the construction site. It looked like the jagged edges of pieces of an aluminum boat, covered with slabs of broken boards.

There was a buzz of conversation about what this whole situation was about. "Who is missing?" someone shouted out. "Oh, no!" was the response of many, as they looked at each other with shock on their faces. The conclusion was that one of the foremen had taken one of the boats out in the middle of the bay and had somehow blown himself up. No one could understand how or why this could have happened.

The rest of the morning people just sat around, unsure about what to do. It was Sunday anyway, so there was no reason to rush off to work. There was also no way of contacting any outside help, as the camp lacked a telephone or radio.

It was ironic, I thought, that the lack of a phone would be one of the selling points of the lodge. The idea was that the tourists would not be bothered by people in the outside world interfering with their relaxation. No one had given much thought to the possibility of an emergency requiring quick medical aid.

Later in the afternoon, we were relieved to see the foreman walk out of the bush into the base camp. He explained that he was sorry for the grief that he had caused everybody. He had apparently become disillusioned with the progress of work at the construction site, especially concerning a dispute with the government agency over funding, and he wanted to stage a demonstration to show his dissatisfaction. He had piled some old lumber in a boat, lit a few sticks of dynamite and pushed the boat out into the middle of the bay. He spent the rest of the morning wandering around in the bush trying to figure out how he would explain his bizarre behaviour.

Leaving Whitewater

As we entered the first week of September, the weather became even colder and wetter, so that few planes could get in. Most of the people huddled around large outdoor fires, rubbing their hands and discussing the predicament. The main problem was that the camp's food supplies were dwindling rapidly, and men were beginning to take time off work to hunt and fish to provide food for their families. Eventually the weather cleared, and I remember the first plane was carrying a load of sliced bread, which was distributed one loaf to each family. We quickly stoked up the fires and began to make toast, eating one slice after another until all the bread was gone.

Families with school-age children were anxious to return to Collins, and there was a steady stream of flights leaving Whitewater Lake over the next few days. The cold, wet weather was closing in again, so a priority departure schedule, of an implicit nature, was started up. This meant that the sick and elderly were allowed to leave first, followed by women and children, older men and so on. I was on just about the last plane to leave the construction site and was the only passenger. Cargo, tools and other supplies destined for Armstrong filled the plane. It took us a while to become airborne, as there was not much of a headwind. The wings teetered back and forth, the flaps extended fully down, and with a loud roar of the motor, we barely cleared the low spruce trees near the shoreline. This turned out to be one of the scariest flights of my life. A light rain rapidly turned to heavy snow. We were suddenly faced with a complete white out, and the pilot, who had no instruments of any kind, not even an altimeter, was at a loss to explain to me where we were. I thought my end would surely come here in this bleak land of swamps and endless coniferous forest. I had sudden glimpses in my mind of crashing and setting up a makeshift camp. Images of a Martin Hartwell (a Yukon pilot who crashed his bush plane and managed to live for many months with both legs broken) type of existence flashed before me.

I looked over at the pilot. He was lost in concentration, peering this way and that, as if there was some peep hole that he had overlooked that would magically restore his vision. "We're going down," he yelled, over the steady roar of the engine. I wondered to my self, "Down? Where to?" The nose of the plane began a gentle, swaying descent. The pilot then sharply pulled up as we began to dangerously skirt over the tops of the trees. "There's an old cutting road around here somewhere," he explained as he motioned with his finger down below. I could see little but a stream of green directly below the plane and a sheet of white above.

It was all pretty harrowing, but before long we flew over the familiar line of railway tracks and began our descent into Caribou Lake near the town of Armstrong. The pilot seemed to have forgotten the adventure before we even landed. He gave no sigh of relief, as one might expect, but began instead to banter about the upcoming weekend. For the pilot, I sensed, experiences such as this one were "business as usual." But for me, it was an entirely different matter. After the pilot left, I sat in the plane for a few minutes, drew in a deep breath, and reflected on this shocking experience. There are times evidently when fieldwork can involve heart pounding adventures and grave risks to one's life. Of course, I started to question why I was doing this research in the first place or what I might be doing wrong when my life was placed in such danger. I could have easily frozen to death on that snowmobile trip to Whitewater Lake with Donald on our visit to Wendel's cabin. Entering the burning Anglican church, with the propane tank in the vestibule, was another dangerous episode. I gave my head a shake and snapped out of my day dreaming. It probably just wasn't my time, yet, I thought and stepped hesitantly out of the plane onto the dock.

Reflections on My Whitewater Fieldwork Experiences

My fieldwork experiences at Whitewater Lake provided me with a unique opportunity to learn how to conduct research in anthropology. My visits with Wendel Beckwith, for example, taught me that you should be "true to your dreams," as Wendel was with his own research and life. I admired Wendel a lot, particularly in the way he was not afraid to think new ideas and follow them through. I see his life in a way as a testament to the value of being different, as a testament to having "the courage of your convictions."

In my own fieldwork, I tried to follow the spirit of Wendel's zest for discovering new ideas and for his enthusiasm about his research. Following Wendel's manner of thinking, I began to see Whitewater Lake as a small laboratory that one could use to experiment with new ideas. My own work on the evolving social organization of the construction camp at Whitewater Lake is a good example of the way my ideas changed and developed.

I came to Whitewater armed with Robert Dunning's study conducted in the 1950s of the Pikangekum Ojibwa community in the Berens River area near the Manitoba border. Dunning had analyzed the composition of hunting families, which he called "co-residential groups," noting that, "The new population grouping is less bound by environmental strictures, and consequently, changing social norms are free to develop more uniformly along lines of a sociological form rather than an environmental control" (1959: 108). My strategy was to use Dunning's observations on Ojibwa social structure as an hypothesis that I could use to initiate my own study of the social groupings at Whitewater Lake. I expected that there would be important differences in the nature of the Ojibwa social organization from Dunning's earlier period to my own, and I intended to use these differences to launch my own analysis. For example, in Dunning's time, the families were mainly fur-trapping units, and the ebb and flow of family life followed the dictates of this economic pursuit. But at Whitewater Lake, there was more mobility in family life because the workers were participants in a wage economy, even though the people still lived in the bush, as at Pikangekum.

I was able to document the forms and shapes of family organization from the ground up, as the family units evolved, with each successive wave of "immigrants" from the Ojibwa communities to the south. Some families quickly located their camp beside one or more other families, while others chose a more isolated location. Thinking about Dunning's phrase about population groupings developing along "lines of a sociological form," I was curious about what sorts of decisions members of families were making when they chose the location for their own campsite. As one might guess, the reasons were quite varied. Some expressed a desire to be with other family members, such as brothers and sisters, while others wanted to be near friends from their home communities. Some people chose their location because they didn't want to be near particular people or because they just wanted to be left alone.

I was able to put together a fairly complete picture of the emerging social organization of the Whitewater camp and to make some reasonable attempts to explain the nature of this emergence, based on several earlier studies of Ojibwa life in northern Ontario. This, then, was my fieldwork strategy. Collect as much accurate information as possible, on a first-hand basis, using whatever techniques seemed most appropriate or were apt to yield the best results, at that time. If it meant being perched up in a tower all day so that I could observe the flow of work activities on the construction site, then that's what I did. I also participated to the extent that I was able or allowed in many of the camp's activities—eating meals with the men, fishing sojourns after work, or chatting it up around a campfire in the evening. Another important part of my research strategy was conducting interviews to obtain first-hand information from workers, crew bosses, the construction foreman, and the women and other family members in the various campsites in the vicinity of the lodge. In other words, I employed primarily the conventional fieldwork methodology of participant-observation supplemented with additional data gathering techniques involving questions and answers.

There was a research design that I also worked on, which evolved over time, so that there was a purpose for the information I was gathering. This design had three primary facets to it—the economic and political strategies, along with their goals and objectives, of the Ogoki River Guides leaders, the economic and organizational facets concerning the construction of the tourist lodge and, lastly, the structure of social life of workers and their families at Whitewater Lake. This overall view of the research with its three-pronged approach allowed me to keep in focus the rational for data collection and, at a later date, integrate the three research areas into a larger theoretical argument or perspective. In my case, the larger plan was to provide a innovative perspective on what is called "patron-client" studies in political anthropology.

In short, the strategy went like this. First, I noticed what I thought were deficiencies in the existing patron-client literature. It was too focused, I argued, on just the so-called leader-follower dyad and on the decision making of each of these participants. On the basis of my studies of similar political activity in Collins involving the Ogoki River Guides organization, I felt that ecological and cultural factors, which were either ignored or hardly discussed in the literature, were important "conditioning elements" of the patron-client relationship. For example, patrons need resources to distribute to followers—where do they get them and how do they use them to their advantage? In cultural terms, the northern Ojibwa view of leadership is that it should be based on important personal qualities, such as generosity, experience as a hunter or being a good family man. Leaders in Collins tended to exemplify these attributes.

This, then, was my planned entry point into the literature. A subtle criticism of existing political studies in anthropology and then demonstrating on the basis of my original fieldwork among the Ojibwa people of northern Ontario that a more sophisticated approach would include ecological and cultural factors in the theoretical analysis of patron-client relationships. It was all put together piece by piece, by reading the anthropological literature with a view on how to improve it, by looking for novel avenues of investigation which I could carry out in my own fieldwork, and then by marshalling the data collected to support the theoretical arguments that would allow for the publication of these studies.

There was also an important personal side to this research, that I was mostly unaware of at the time, but that has had the effect of changing me as a person. On the basis of these experiences at Whitewater Lake, I became less likely to get upset by life's "trials and tribulations." When I am struggling with some aspect of my life, I think for a moment about how the Ojibwa people up in the bush country of northern Ontario also struggle, with less resources at their disposal than I have. They carry on with acceptance and dignity, rarely complaining about their lot in life.

While my research in Nipigon country involved some difficulties, these were endured for only a relatively short period of time. I always had the option to leave if I wished and had the means to do so. This is not much of an option for the Native people themselves. Whatever hardships I suffered were not to be tolerated for my whole life, as is the case with northern residents. The trials that were a part of my research are part of a life-long process for northern people. The hardships are many for these people—planes crash, people are burnt in house fires, freeze in snow banks, are hit by trains and live at an economic level that southern Ontario residents would hardly tolerate. I don't mean to sound smug in any way, but research in the northern bush country not only allows the fieldworker to begin to appreciate life on life's terms in the northern locale but also to appreciate the benefits of living in the south. Overall, one might say that fieldwork engenders a better awareness of life in general because we are able to see our own life's path in a larger, more comparative perspective.

Chapter Six

Spirituality: The Hidden Reality

… the darkness made them invisible to me, but their presence remained strong as their prayers joined the mix of chants, whistles and rattles in the steamy air.… There was a joining together of other spirits in common survival and common re-dedication, an intertwining in voice, experience, thought and determination. It was hard not to feel a spiritual closeness. —Rupert Ross (1992: 179)

It took me quite a while to realize that fieldwork involves a multi-faceted process of investigation. By "multi-faceted" I mean that there are many different dimensions to how we perceive "reality." In the beginning phase of my fieldwork, it was relatively easy to talk with people about their family and kinship ties. Economic and political matters were a little more difficult to delve into, probably because these matters are more private than the "public" domain of family relationships. In time, as people became more familiar with me and my investigation, they were more willing to talk about their hunting, their incomes or their views on leadership. It was partly a matter of the people's familiarity with me and partly a willingness on my part to push my investigation deeper into the realities of social and material life.

I was content for the most part with confining my investigation to matters of the material world, the economic and political stuff. It was only near the latter stages of the fieldwork that I began to perceive the importance of a whole other reality, another dimension to life that I had hitherto either ignored or was incapable of perceiving. I was living in the midst of an entirely different world, what you might call a "spiritual reality," and I never realized it.

Eyes of the Thunderbird

Fieldwork requires periods of reflection. For my part, I used to go for long walks on the trails through the surrounding forest or along the railway tracks. On one of those hot muggy days in August, in the later afternoon, I ventured out on the railway tracks with the intention of taking a short stroll to clear my mind and to think about a few other angles to the community study that I was immersed in.

The tracks out of the village going west pursue a straight course for about a quarter of a mile, then take a sharp bend through a rock cut. I had been this way many times before, and my mind began drifting in a general sort of way about the peculiarities of fieldwork in anthropology, about how difficult it is at times to keep focused on what you're doing, especially when this work requires that you to be "on duty," or at least on call, virtually twenty-four hours a day. After several minutes of this sort of meditation, I was startled to hear a sharp crack of thunder. It seemed so close, clear and crisp, as if it were just overhead. I also thought to myself, "How strange, the sky is still pretty clear." There didn't appear to be any threat of rain. Suddenly a sharp bolt of lightening struck several yards in front of me, hitting the steel rails of the tracks. This was followed in quick succession by several more bolts, also hitting the rails, as if they were acting like a lightening rod. I ran forward, stopped, then ran again, fearful that I would be struck at any second. It must be the way foot soldiers feel when bombarded by artillery. You just never knew where it was coming from or whether you would be the next victim.

It soon became apparent to me that running down the tracks was a bad idea, so I veered sharply to the left, heading for a bush trail that I remembered led back to the village. The rain started at this point, striking my back in big, splattering blobs. What was even more strange was the ferocity with which I was now attacked by mosquitoes. It was like they had received a message that I was to be their last meal. The biting insects spurred me to run faster. My wet shirt laid bare my skin, and this seemed to invigorate their desire for blood. The leaves and branches along the trail whipped my face as I ran through them, leaving welts and scratches all over my upper body. It didn't take long for the rain to stop, for the biting bugs to return to their hiding places and for the sun to break through the clouds. It all happened so quickly that I began to wonder if had occurred at all. I had all these mosquito bites, which by now were becoming very itchy, but there was hardly any outward appearance of a storm.

By the time I reached the village, I could see columns of smoke rising from several of the buildings. Over at the schoolroom, beside the store, the chimney had been blown to bits, leaving a smouldering pile of tin. At Donald's cabin down by the lake, the chimney suffered a similar fate. When I went inside to look around, I found Elizabeth, his elderly mother, cowering in the corner, quite visibly shaken by the incident. Donald told me that the older people in the village are all afraid because they believe that the attack was initiated by the thunderbird and that the lightening is directed from his eyes. This was a sign, he related, of great impending doom. Someone in the village must have done something of immense wrong to have brought on such misfortune, and the old woman was waiting "for the other foot to fall."

The whole incident had unnerved me as well. Without any of the usual indications of a natural phenomenon, one could only conclude that there were supernatural forces at work here. But what was the basis for it all? The explanation about the thunderbird seemed eminently reasonable to me, because I had never seen anything like this before.

In the lore of the Ojibwa of the Nipigon area there are two varieties of thunderbird. One of them is thought to have a bad temper and is apt to destroy people with its lightening. The other is a more benevolent sort of creature, with a milder temperament, whose thunder is much quieter. In early spring, when the thunderbirds return from their homes in the south, offerings of tobacco are made to them. This is thought to placate them, so that the birds will protect, rather than harm, the people. The nests of the thunderbird are believed to be located atop a large mountain out in Lake Nipigon and are made of stones. The top of this mountain is blanketed with clouds, which disguises the nests' exact locations. When hydro-electric dams were constructed on the southern parts of Lake Nipigon in the 1940s, it was believed by the Ojibwa people that white men had learned how to capture the power of the thunderbird. They enticed the birds to shoot their lightening down to earth, where it was captured inside pipes and converted into electrical power. This harassment of the thunderbird caused them to destroy their large stone nests in Lake Nipigon, and the blanket of clouds disappeared from the sacred mountain.

I couldn't help reflect later on the allegoric content of this thunderbird episode. It is hard to ignore the parallel between the subversion of the thunderbirds' power by the Euro-Canadian society to feed its voracious need for hydro-electric power, on the one hand, and the general subjugation of First Nations society by whites on the other. Both Natives and the thunderbirds have suffered the same fate, which is an emasculation of their ability to control their own destiny in life.

It is perhaps ironic, though, that the thunderbird continues to haunt the Native psyche, occasionally demonstrating an ability for an awesome outburst of power. The thunderbirds live on, beyond traditional times, in the hidden reality of the spirit world, demonstrating their continued vitality and penchant for destructiveness for those who might have forgotten about their existence.

Nanabozo, the Sleeping Giant

The allegoric nature of Ojibwa spirituality was brought home to me on several other occasions during the course of my fieldwork. On an unusually hot day during the spring, I had gone for a stroll along a trail that winds its way along the shoreline of Collins Lake and then circles back through a series of cabins. People were particularly active on this day, which is what happens when your energy levels have been suppressed through the long winter months of confinement. You feel exhilarated and want to get outside and do things. At one cabin, for example, an older couple had just set up a woodstove in front of their cabin. Many people cook outside during the summer, with an idea similar to our barbecue, to keep the inside of their house cool. Other people were raking up the winter's debris and burning the brush in small, aromatic piles of leaves and twigs.

Near the end of this trail of cabins, I noticed four or five men sitting on a pile of freshly peeled logs. They had begun an addition to a cabin, which was now up three or four feet. Apparently in no hurry to work very hard, they just sat there enjoying the sunshine. Several of the men, I noticed, were playing with small branches, stripping the bark off, discarding it, then reaching down for another. One of these fellows called me over. I recognized him and another younger man sitting beside him from my tree planting days about five years before. These two knew me in a work-related context, rather than as an anthropologist doing fieldwork, so there was a certain comraderie that I shared with them that was different from the relationship I had with the others.

"Do you remember, Ed, when we used to work up at Kakebeka," he said, motioning me over, "and you kept bugging us all the time to tell you those old stories." I chose a log to sit on, steadying it so it wouldn't roll off the pile. He turned the other men, "He always thought we were 'B.S.ing' him, but we weren't. These were the things the old people told us when we were kids. Right?" looking over their way for a sign of agreement.

"That story about the Sleeping Giant. Remember?" he continued, "I bet you thought that I just made that up, didn't you?" The others smiled and laughed a little, which I took to mean there was some "B.S.ing" that went on from time to time. The storyteller made a slight facial expression of disapproval at this suggestion, but he pushed on.

"The Sleeping Giant is our Nanabozo, I think you know that, but did you know that he created the earth and human beings?" he paused, taking a breath. "There are a lot of details here that would take days to tell, but we have to get back to work sometime," so he continued to relate the Nanabozo story.

Nanabozo is the Ojibwa's hero, the central figure in their mythology. He was the first person on earth, brother of *Maheegun* the wolf, part human, but with supernatural powers. The Nanabozo story can take on epic proportions, if one had the time to listen to it all, which these people did during their winters on the trapline and hunting camps. The gist of the story is that Nanabozo saved life on this earth, which they call Turtle Island, during the time of a great flood. All of the animals were just floating around clinging to logs and clumps of brush. Nanabozo summoned together all of the aquatic animals and sent them down under the water to find some earth. One by one the great swimmers—the otter, beaver, and so on—failed in their quest, until the lowly muskrat managed to accomplish the task. Completely exhausted, achieving this feat through sheer force of determination, he surfaced with a small chunk of soil in his claws. From this bit of earth, Nanabozo fashioned a patch of ground that he magically kept enlarging until it was big enough for all of the creatures of the forest. He sent various birds off in all directions, but they kept coming back, so Nanabozo continued to increase the size of the earth until the birds no longer returned.

At this point in the story we are told that Nanabozo, having accomplished this great feat, becomes bored and seeks a companion to join him in life. He begins to fashion a person like himself out of clay, which he puts in a fire to harden it. In the first attempt, the figure is too light in colour, so he discards it and tries again. This second time, the clay figure is burnt too much and it is similarly thrown away. Finally, on the third attempt, a figure that is the right shade of brown is retrieved from the fire. Nanabozo breathes life into this figure and thereby creates the first human being.

After this story of creation, the tale unfolds in many directions. There is an episode, for example, when the waters of Lake Nipigon had dried up because it had been swallowed by giant snakes. Nanabozo battled these snakes, eventually puncturing them, one by one, until the water in the lake was restored to its original level. On another occasion he is spying on some young maidens who had gone down to the lake to fetch some water. In order to disguise himself, Nanabozo squeezes himself into a hollow log but becomes stuck in it. As he tried to wiggle loose, the girls heard the commotion and went to investigate. They then realized that Nanabozo had plotted to peek on them. Displeased with this unwanted intrusion on their privacy and finding Nanabozo stuck in his hiding place, they proceeded to beat him about the head and poke him with pointed sticks.

One of these stories is my favourite of all, because it so aptly illustrates Nanabozo's capacity for ineptitude, despite his miraculous powers. Nanabozo, it is said, was hunting ducks one day when he managed to bag many more than he could possibly eat at one time. After building a fire and enjoying a good meal, he buried the ducks so that other predators wouldn't find them. The trouble was that Nanabozo needed to find them later, so he buried the ducks in the sand along a beach with their feet just barely sticking up. As luck would have it, a fox had been secretly watching Nanabozo and was therefore aware of his contrivance to hide the ducks. One by one, the fox ate the ducks but being more clever than Nanabozo, the duck's feet were placed back in the sand to make it appear as if the cache was still intact. Now, since Nanabozo did not need to eat very often, he would come by the beach every so often to check on his ducks. Seeing that they were still in their uprighted position he assumed, of course, that his next meal was safely tucked away. When the time came, though, to enjoy his quarry, he soon found out that he had been tricked. Now, hungry and angry, he stomped around berating himself for his stupidity.

The story of the adventures of Nanabozo is an epic tale, akin to Homer's *Iliad*, describing the siege of Troy, or the *Odyssey*, recounting Ulysses' wanderings in the ancient world. In addition, what is especially peculiar to me about Nanabozo as a heroic figure are his personal foibles. He is clumsy around women and possesses an almost humourous inability to see the faults in his grand designs and plans. Nanabozo has abilities which are prodigious in their magnitude yet at times exhibits a naivety that is more child-like than would be expected from one with such talents.

I am led to believe, though, that the entertainment value of the Nanabozo narrative is considered by the Ojibwa to be of secondary importance to its moral or instructive content. The Nanabozo epic is two narratives running side by side. There is the "surface" narrative of Nanabozo's life and adventures. This narrative is entertaining in its own right, filled with all the ingredients of a good story—humour, pathos and irony. But under the surface is the moral ingredient about proper attitudes and behaviour, about how people should live their life in the northern bush. For example, even the best hunter should not take himself too seriously. We are all prone to make mistakes. To correct them by altering our behaviour is the key to success. Humour takes the hard edge off the reality of the hunting way of life with its precarious food supply. Above all, an arrogant hunter is doomed to failure, subjecting himself, his family and all those other people who depend on him to possible starvation and misery. In an allegoric sense, we are all Nanabozo and should learn to live like him.

Bear Stories

It wasn't too long after this recounting of the life and times of Nanabozo that a young man, a student, came to talk to me about some of the things that happened to him when he was a child. There was the usual feeling-out process to ascertain how sensitive I was to First Nations beliefs and culture. He talked about growing up in the woods in a small log cabin with his younger brothers and sisters. For whatever reason, these children were raised by their grandparents, and there seemed to be no end to the supernatural phenomena that occurred in and around their cabin. The student's grandfather was a shaman, who, I gathered from the young man's story, was responsible for attracting these "other than usual" occurrences. The children were constantly told to be on guard for strange creatures, for people who might look at them in an odd way or for objects out of the usual that they might find along the path to their cabin. This was all pretty general stuff up to now, but the student became more serious.

"One evening all of us, my grandparents and brothers and sisters, were just sitting around after supper when all of a sudden a large ball of fire, or lightening, burst through the front door of the cabin. We were all horrified and scampered back to the inner walls as the ball whirled about, making several turns, before it disappeared through the window. We just stood there for a long time, afraid to move," he explained. He accompanied his story with dramatic gestures, whirling his hands around in circles to depict the fire ball.

You could tell that he was quite sincere in relating this story, because his eyes revealed a certain shocked look, as if he were now reliving the event. The strange occurrences, he related further, were typical of the so-called "medicine fights" that his grandfather was involved in with other shamen in distant locals. Shortly after the fire-ball incident, his grandfather encountered a large bear walking upright towards him down the trail to their cabin. In hushed tones, the young man let me know that this was no "real" bear, because when a bear walks upright for a long period of time, you know that inside of it is the spirit of another human being—an evil medicine man.

"My grandfather attacked this bear creature with an axe," he said, making a downward chopping motion with his hand to make the point, "splitting his skull open. We learned later that this old man in a far away village died about the same time, so that was probably him who was sending us this bad medicine," he related, again with a lowered voice and serious tone.

I have always found this matter of the role of the bear in the northern Native psyche an interesting matter. In Collins, I used to wonder why bear meat was not greatly desired, even though, in economic terms, bears provide the highest proportion of edible meat per animal next to the moose. Although they are fairly numerous in the Lake Nipigon area, bears are not usually hunted but are shot when they become a nuisance to the village. While some people claim to eat bear meat, others say they avoid it because a skinned bear looks too much like a human being. Some also say that bear meat should be smoked because if it is eaten fresh it will cause diarrhoea. The idea here is not that the bear meat itself causes this ailment, it is because the bear is a sacred animal and, accordingly, one should avoid eating too much of such creatures. While it is not readily admitted, the attribution of anthropomorphic characteristics to the bear could be taken as evidence of the widespread magico-religious mystique associated with the bear in the northern hemisphere. This mystique is probably a reflection of the fact that both bears and humans occupy a similar ecological niche—they are both omnivores, scavenging sorts of creatures—that are apt at times to come into conflict with one another. This could happen, for example, at berry picking time in the fall or during the fish runs in the spring. Bears are also thought be very intelligent creatures, which might account for the notion that bears and people are "brothers" in some respects. I also occasionally saw large bear skins stretched out on frames outside people's cabins which, since the skins are not sold or used as rugs, I took to be an attempt to ward off other bears.

I had my own encounter with a couple of bears, which I found quite unnerving, yet instructive. It was a habit of mine to take time away from the life in the village by going on short hunting trips. This was in the fall when people were out in the bush wondering around, and so were the bears. I would borrow a .22 rifle and head out to the stands of deciduous trees to hunt for partridge. The leaves had mostly fallen by now, although the weather was still warm. As I walked along the trail, I listened intently for the faint rustling sound of the birds' feet as they scratched around looking for things to eat. Off in the distance I could hear the loud "thwap, thwap," like an outboard motor, as a male partridge beat its wings against a log as part of their mating ritual.

All of a sudden I heard a different noise. It was coming toward me, softly, sounding sort of fluffy, "woosh, woosh." I looked up just in time to see a huge snowy owl, with a wingspan of about four or five feet, trying to dive bomb me. Its large claws, dangling dangerously below it, opened as if to grab hold of the top of my skull. I dove face first onto the ground and quickly turned to see this large lumbering bird making its slow ascent over the trees behind me. I was never too sure whether it was just trying to scare me, like warding off an intruder, or if it really meant to do me some harm. I suspected that this huge bird was quite capable of doing whatever it pleased with the top of my head.

It took me several hours of strolling around to shake off the effects of this strange encounter. I kept looking over my shoulder to see if something else was coming at me from behind. It was probably for this reason that I wasn't paying too much attention in front of me to see where I was going. At one point, the trail made a sharp L-turn on an elevated patch of ground overlooking a large lake below, and quite suddenly I was nose-to-nose with a mother bear and her cub. I knew that this situation meant a lot of trouble for me, as the mother bear would do anything to protect her cub.

I looked down at my .22 rifle and realized that this was a pretty useless weapon in such a situation. It all happened so fast that the bear apparently still didn't know where I was. It just sniffed around, in an agitated fashion, wondering where this strange smell was coming from. I was just frozen stiff, knowing that the slightest movement could spell disaster. If I turned and ran, the bear would surely dart out after me, and they can run faster that most people, I am told. Even though the bear was no more than a few feet away from me, I don't think she ever actually saw me. She just sniffed around some more and eventually made a slow descent down into the valley below towards the lake. I could do nothing more than just stare at them in amazement, with my feet rooted in the ground. I was thinking all along that if I could just keep my cool, without panicking, the bears would find no harm in me. For whatever reason it worked, much to my relief even to this day.

The older generation of Anishenabe (Ojibwa), if they met a bear in the bush, would stop and talk to it. They would address the bear as "Our grandfather" and then watch for movements of the bear's ears and head as an indication that it understood. It is thought that if a bear were addressed properly, with the appropriate supplicatory remarks, it would no longer be angry and would release its hold on one. The bones of a bear were shown great respect. Bear skulls were occasionally decorated with ribbons and paint and hung in trees. Smaller bones were utilized as charms or as instruments in medicinal rites.

There are also stories about people who had certain special dreams about bears. This was at the time of a young person's medicine dream or, in more general terms, of the *manitou-kauso* or vision quest. The bear would appear to this person and say that it would be its guardian in life. The guardian would look after the person, protecting them from harm and giving them special powers. This bear-spirit would also say that the young person must show respect for the bear and never kill it. At the end of these instructions, the bear would enter into the body of the dreamer. As the young person grew up, they would therefore believe that there was a bear hidden inside their body. This "bear-in-the-body" phenomenon, however, could cause great distress. If an evil conjurer wanted to injure such a person, say for purposes of revenge, the bear inside the person could be poisoned, causing sickness or death. A hollow bear bone could also be used to try and suck out this sickness, but it probably would not be successful if the evil conjurer's medicine was too strong.

The Ojibwa of the northern forests are a peaceful people, generally, and are not usually prone to outward acts of aggression or violence. One is at first struck by their patience, laughter and self-control. It is common to find people freely sharing their possessions or families cooperating in all kinds of ventures. They do this with good humour and a genuine feeling of love for their fellow human beings. It is this "caring-for-others" attitude that I personally found so remarkable among the Ojibwa people that I met in the Lake Nipigon area. However, there are also certain other deeper psychological realities of Native life.

One is apt to wonder about how the problems of latent hostilities that all human societies face are dealt with if no overt manifestation of these troubles are allowed in face-to-face interaction. The cordiality in interpersonal relations that is so evident in everyday life, one suspects, has a counterpart in the deeper functioning of social affairs. If open hostility is discouraged and self-restraint the expected rule of social behaviour, then it would be reasonable to seek an indirect mechanism for the discharge of aggressive tendencies.

This indirect means of venting, or resolving, strains in the social fabric of the community is why, I believe, the people resort to supernatural avenues as a covert and indirect, yet nonetheless aggressive, means for evening up such personal slights as insults, gossip and various other causes of latent hostilities. The Ojibwa people are not allowed by their moral code to openly quarrel with others, but magic and sorcery are socially sanctioned institutions for venting anger.

Ruth Landes, an anthropologist who lived with members of the Manitou Rapids Indian Band in the 1930s, wrote that their chief was "so feared that few shamans dared to enter shamanistic combat with him when he insulted them with slighting remarks." Landes continues:

> Influential persons who are known or suspected to be sorcerers are recognized in more general ways than in being deferred to professionally. People cower physically before them, shrink away, hush their talk, straighten their faces lest the shaman suspect some intended offense in their behavior.... One boy became paralysed shortly after the shaman chose to be offended by his careless laugh. It is perfectly consistent with this attitude that laughing, particularly on the part of women, is not loud but light. Paralysis, incontinence, twisted mouth, and the windigo insanity are sent by shamans who have been offended by casual behavior. The shaman's exquisite sensitiveness to slights, real or imaginary, is intelligible to the people because it is only an accentuation of the sensitiveness felt by every person. (1937b: 113–14)

Of course this covert use of magical force raises all sorts of other problems, maybe more than it actually solves, because one can never be sure who is or is not in the process of poisoning or otherwise harming you in some way. Any injury or ill health is apt to lead to a search for previous social slights that could have triggered the hostilities of another person. Under the masks of cordiality could lurk the evil intent of a conjurer. The belief that other human beings might be doing you harm in a covert way could lead to all sorts of unconscious hostilities. Dreams are gone over in meticulous detail in a search for the clues or signs that one's inner privacy is being invaded for malevolent intentions. This can lead to an abnormal concern with personal introspection on the one hand and latent suspicion of people on the other.

There is no easy solution, in social-structural terms, to this sort of problem in human society, except for people to try to keep on good terms with their neighbours. In fact, this could well be a pretty fair functionalist explanation for the resolution of interpersonal conflicts in societies, such as northern hunting and gathering ones, in which cordial social relations could be a very prerequisite of survival. The use of conjurers to fight one's battles removes an interpersonal hostility above the level of the everyday, natural world, into a new, ethereal plane of existence. The battles there are unpredictable, even capricious, in their outcome, making people wary of offending others. Cordiality and cooperation are thus promoted below, while epic magical contests are waged above. Both the gods and the people would appear to be happy with the continuance of this arrangement.

Exploring the Hidden Reality

Fieldwork involves penetrating different levels of reality. Perhaps the word "level" is not an entirely appropriate term, because it implies some sort of hierarchy. Probably what I mean is that there exists a hidden dimension to fieldwork that may be only partially perceived and partly experienced by the ethnographer. Even in a community like Collins, the people themselves have different perceptions of the supernatural world, depending on their age, personal experiences, what was taught to them by their elders, and the like. As with other cultural phenomena, though, there is no doubt a sharing within the community of supernatural knowledge. Any investigation on the part of a fieldworker into this hidden dimension of people's lives is a more difficult matter than the more conventional research into the material and social parts of life. People may not want to appear unsophisticated, superstitious or backward to the university-educated anthropologist. People may also wish to guard their inner views on supernatural matters lest they be open to ridicule. These factors, and more, can hamper research into supernatural beliefs.

It is as if life exists, or is experienced, on two separate planes of reality— the mental or spiritual and the physical. This "hidden world" of spiritual beliefs and symbolic systems for most is apt to be only dimly perceived, if at all, by the researcher. Normal methods of investigation, such as the interview, might be all but useless, as people will probably shy away from direct questioning procedures. Tact during casual conversation is likely to elicit more information. This is what occurred during my conversation concerning the *cheebuy* (ghost), as talked about earlier. A community member wondered whether I had seen Ed Pigeon's ghost. Perhaps he only wanted to know if, by seeing the ghost myself, I was able to participate in his spiritual reality. Steve had stayed in my cabin for several nights, when I was away buying groceries at Savant Lake, before this conversation about ghosts occurred, and I felt at the time that he was trying to reciprocate in some way. There are always matters that you wish you had pursued further in your fieldwork, and this is one of them. I wasn't really interested in *cheebuy*; in fact, I was a bit concerned that if I started to see Ed Pigeon's apparition floating around my cabin at night that this could preoccupy me in some way that could ruin my fieldwork.

I realized I was on touchy ground here. I wanted to participate in the world of the Collins' people, but I was trying to restrict the investigation to material or physical matters—economics, leadership and the like. There was a separate reality out there that I didn't want to get involved in; as a way of insulating myself, I allowed some things in, but kept others out. I wanted to prevent an erosion of my academic, theoretical, ethnographic modes of thinking. I wasn't consciously aware of this protectionism, but when I look back at the situation that occurred with Elijah's funeral procession, I see my lack of involvement as an excuse to avoid becoming too conceptually captivated by the inscrutable world of spirituality.

The degree to which we are able to allow ourselves to take chances in fieldwork is a personal matter, but I suspect that those who are willing to cast aside the insulating blanket of their own cultural constructs may be in a more opportune position to experience the "other reality" that is in the minds of their informants. It wasn't very often that people in Collins would come forward on their own, as Steve did, to volunteer information to me on such sensitive matters as ghosts and the afterlife. Don't get me wrong, I didn't avoid the subject altogether. We did talk about Pigeon's ghost for some time, but only in a light, humorous sort of way. Why Steve should think that I would see this ghost over behind the woodstove, I cannot say. Perhaps over the last several nights he himself had seen the apparition, and it was near the stove that he had witnessed it. If this was the case, it apparently didn't startle Steve enough to scare him away from my cabin. When I think about it now, the ghost of Ed Pigeon was probably something that Steve would actually expect to see—if he wasn't there, that might be considered unusual. Maybe, too, others, such as Sogo Sabosans who actually owned the cabin and was letting me stay there, had seen the ghost as well. I did feel a certain camaraderie with Steve for this sharing of experience, even though these "sharings" were not based all that much on a mutual understanding of each other's concepts of spirituality.

For that matter, I don't even know if a literal translation of the Ojibwa "*cheebuy*" as "ghost" is appropriate. It implies a mutual, overlapping of conceptual territory that I should not presume actually exists. In an earlier period of anthropology, back in the 1960s, there were a lot of papers on cognitive anthropology, or "ethno-science" as it was sometimes called, that postulated huge difficulties in transposing the "conceptual domains" from one culture to another.

These conceptual difficulties also bring to the forefront the larger philosophical or methodological issues about how we perceive "reality" in our own culture, never mind anyone else's. Handle this conundrum any way you want, but for my purpose, I am willing to begin by conceding, first, that life takes place on two planes of existence. On one plane is the physical world which we perceive through our senses. We smell the freshness of wind blowing off a northern lake, we see a hawk drifting overhead, or feel the ache in our bones caused by the winter's cold. The mental plane can be every much as "real," even when it comes to sensing sounds, sights and feelings. But it seems that there is a wider scope involved in this other plane of existence. We can travel, for example, through time and space in our thoughts and dreams in ways not possible in the ordinary physical plane. Our imagination allows for the construction of a reality without bounds in the ordinary, mundane sense of life. In our minds, we can become the soaring hawk or the breeze off the lake.

The question here, having to do with fieldwork in Collins, is about understanding the Ojibwa concept of the spiritual plane and how it might have evolved over time. In other words, is there a relationship between adaptation in the physical world of the hunter-gatherer life and the evolution of mental constructs whose changes could work in concert with the adaptive process to the physical mode of existence? My contention here is that the two planes of existence do not constitute dual, separate realities but an intertwining of the physical and mental, where changes in one circle back to effect changes in the other.

In this light, spirituality and the wide corpus of symbolic belief systems work in concert with one another. It is not just that one world is "real" and the other is not, for the physical and the mental are both constructs of a human mind imbued with the shapes and forms of cultural life. Rupert Ross, a lawyer in the Kenora district of northwestern Ontario, has expressed the matter in a particularly cogent manner:

> To many Native people, the spiritual plane is not simply a sphere of activity or belief which is separate from the pragmatics of everyday life; instead, it seems to be a context from within which most aspects of life are seen, defined and given significance. (1992: 54–55)

Ross' exploration of spirituality in northern Ontario suggests that the emergence of this reality in historical terms can be understood as an aspect of survival in a hunter-gatherer context. In other words, traditional times were survival times, survival by small family groups alone in the wilderness. This reality of food shortages and even starvation, when people lived and died depending on their own skills, luck and fate, can therefore be understood as providing the conditions for the way the mind must work in order to enhance a survival strategy.

Life for the Cree and Ojibwa in the northern forests was lived to a large extent at the mercy of the elements. Long winter snowstorms could prevent hunting, forcing people to huddle together in their tents, becoming ever colder and weaker. Summer was a more abundant time, but rainstorms could curtail hunting and fishing as well. Native people lived at the mercy not only of the elements, but furthermore, at the mercy of the spirits which controlled these elements. Religious ideology and mode of production are therefore interrelated phenomena in subarctic Native life (i.e., Hedican 1995: 115–121; Ridington 1988; Rogers 1962; Tanner 1979). The "masters of the animals," for example, give and take away the availability of game, depending on the rituals of respect and a proper observance of hunting etiquette.

In this cultural and ecological context, knowledge of the spiritual or mental plane of existence is probably more crucial to a group's survival than abilities in the physical realm, such as tracking skills or knowledge of fish and animal habits. A hunter's skill is useless if it cannot be applied, if the animal spirits refuse to release the game for human consumption. In an existential sense, therefore, it is not the spirit world that is depended upon the world of physical reality, but the other way around. Life in the subarctic forest is predicated on an ability to interact in propitious ways with the supernatural entities that make human life possible.

Because the people lived at the mercy of the spirit world, this probably made them guarded in any discussions with an outsider about the supernatural world. The risks of upsetting the "balance of nature," of displeasing the spirits, are too great when survival is at stake. Of course there is humanitarian aid that makes starvation in northern Canada unlikely today, but still, there is a strong tendency for culturally-defined views of the universe to endure, propelled forward by the weight of tradition.

Chapter Seven

Back at McGill

Of what value is comment by friends, if it is not honest, and you know
that it is honest if it says some things that are unpalatable at first. —
Cree politician, in R. Salisbury (1986: 156)

Out of the Bush

On the day that I finally left Collins, with my worn packsack and collection of
roped-up cardboard boxes, it was a cold November morning. I had said my
goodbyes the night before, although no one wanted to let on that I was leaving.
"Oh, we'll see you again, soon enough," they said. It was their way of dealing
with the pain of departure and separation, I reasoned. It was something I had
noticed before; Collins people just left, whether for a few hours or forever,
without saying much about it. There might be a quick handshake or an older
woman wiping away a tear, but no large hugs or other outward displays of
emotion. The people were just as reserved about going away as they were about
everything else. "Is this apparent stoicism just them, who they are, or is it an
adaptive social trait that helps cope with life in the northern bush?" I wondered.

At five in the morning a bunch of us stood alongside the railway tracks
waiting for the passenger train to Armstrong. Women held their babies in the
tikanagans, or cradle boards, covered over with shawls. Steam billowed up into
the cool air from the babies' warm breath under their coverings.

The train rumbled along, without too much of a wait. It is always such a
relief to see it coming down the tracks; soon we would be warm and comfortable,
with the Collins' cabins, smoke streaming in upward spirals, quickly receding
behind us. The trip to Armstrong is a short journey, usually only taking a half
hour or so. I had previously made arrangements for a ride to Thunder Bay with
a friend, and he was waiting outside the station when the train pulled up. The
drive to "The Lakehead," as the local people call the city, takes about three
hours over a gravelly, somewhat bumpy road. My friend dropped me off at the
airport, and by the middle of the afternoon, I was aboard a plane to Toronto,
then over to Montreal.

I took a cab downtown from the Dorval airport, and it brought me to
Sherbrooke Street near McGill. And then, all of a sudden, it hit me—an intense
feeling of confusion and disorientation. I had started the day in the quiet
environment of Ontario's northern bush. The rush-hour traffic along Sherbrooke
seemed like a deafening roar to me; I longed for the solitude of my little cabin.
I looked down at myself. My jeans were pretty dirty, but I hadn't noticed it this

morning. My packsack and collection of boxes must have been looked down upon by the smartly dressed women and men on their way home from the office buildings nearby. An intense feeling of dislocation, of being out of place, of not belonging to life here in the city, overwhelmed me. It had happened too quickly, this journey from my log cabin to the urban screech of Montreal. There was no transition period. I was just there, far too quickly for my mind to adjust.

I knew, though, that my fieldwork in Collins had actually begun back at McGill in Montreal, so it was all right for me to return here. It was here in Montreal that the project was first conceptualized, talked about with students and professors and researched in the library. It was here that grants were secured for the travel and other expenses. The project therefore must end here as well, where I would have the time to gather my thoughts and research material and begin to write it all up.

In this sense, fieldwork has a circular movement to it, like the changing of the seasons—getting started, doing the fieldwork, surviving and departure. I had not set an agenda for when I would leave the Collins-Armstrong-Whitewater Lake area. I figured that the time would be right when I started to get repetitive, when my books on various facts and figures were filled up, and when I ceased to feel the challenge of discovery. When I left, I knew that I would be back, quite a few times as it turned out, so there was no tear-gushing farewell involved. That's one of the advantages of not being too far from home. You can do a reasonable job at keeping up with things. But fieldwork does need closure. It needs to be packaged in a certain intellectual sense which helps one see it in an analyzable, objective perspective.

When I was living in my little cabin back in the northern woods, Montreal and the people back at McGill sometimes seemed an eternity away. I conditioned myself, though, to keep mentally "in touch" so that I didn't drift away completely. There was only a remote possibility of "going native," but nonetheless I was guarded against feeling too comfortable in my little remote world. In fact there were certain exercises that I carried out, prepping myself for the time when I would have to go back and defend my ideas in seminars and group discussions. Articles for publication and maybe even a book were goals that I kept in mind. My little exercises involved keeping a notebook in which I listed all of the topics that my pieces of fieldwork would fit into. I was thinking here of general headings, such as work and occupations, kinship and residence patterns, and leadership roles and attitudes. With these headings it was much easier to see where you might be short on some area of data collection or how certain ideas naturally grouped together with some others. It was much easier to manipulate these various headings and titles than to deal directly with all that so-called "raw data."

As I keep reiterating over again, fieldwork is primarily a learning experience for the ethnographer, as much as it is a more academic, research task. Like riding a bicycle, it takes time to get your balance, to know how to handle the pot holes and finally to be confident enough to lift your head up so you can smell the breeze. While in Collins, the reality of what I was doing was kept intact primarily by my mentor, Richard Salisbury, professor of anthropology. Occasionally he would write to me, ostensibly to keep me up on the comings and goings back at McGill, but more to keep track of my academic progress with his "gentle reminders."

Gentle Reminders

July 4th

Dear Ed,

I enjoyed your note of June 13th, commenting on differences in views of development, and on the delay of the tourist lodge project until October. I hope the money lasts, but it sounds fine for the project.

I would add a gentle reminder about the possible usefulness of reports. You obviously have ideas about (a) different perceptions of development, (b) the role of leaders, their perceptions and followers' perceptions, and (c) the organization of productive tasks. Are you sure you are writing those ideas down? Are you discussing them with people in the field? One month from now will you remember how your thinking developed now, so that you could trace out that development? Are you confident you have the right data to be able to support your ideas in the arena of a seminar paper, or discussion with colleagues. All of these questions, if you answer "no" to any of them, suggests to me that writing down in a very preliminary form what you are thinking and formalising would assist you in many ways. (All quite apart from the very practical aspect that it enables me to feel reassured that all is going well, and for me to pass on the reassurance to the Department, to students like Bob, Charlie, and Bill, and to funding agencies).

At the minimum I am suggesting that sitting down and "talking" to paper (at a time like when it is raining, or when you feel depressed) and trying to think abstractly about the practical reality which you are very tightly involved in, is useful in focusing your work as you go along. It is very easy to get right out of academic, theoretical thinking completely. Discussing with people in the field is one way of getting feedback and criticism; sending those written thoughts to a (?) sympathetic reader for comment is another way. The replies which come back weeks later are not always useful, but in writing down for an audience you do realise where you need data and ask yourself why you do particular things. You get your own ideas straight. I keep all letters on file if you want them back as evidence of events or theoretical ideas and their emergence after the fieldwork (it reduces the risk of loss to you, should your canoe capsize, etc). So much for a gentle hint. I realise that everyone works differently, so it is just a suggestion; at least try some data analysis in the field, whether you announce the fact or not. Like the intensity of domestic production?

Things go quietly and smoothly here. I haven't yet gone north this summer, although one of our boys, John, is camping and canoeing north of Temagami this summer. Bob is collecting his data in St. John's on how developers think, before going to Labrador in August for the other side. Charlie has made a number of new Rasta contacts in New York and has optimistic prospects now, without having to go to the UK—though his last letter spoke feelingly about the heat. Heavens knows what it must be like in NY with the garbage men on strike again. Bill had to give up on Argentina for all sorts of reasons including political ones; they are planning to do a similar study of stagnating "satellised" mining areas in Canada instead—which would probably begin when their baby arrives in a month or two. Liz takes off for a month in Las Vegas on July 18th, while Jeanette is quitting in early August.

Good Luck, and I hope to hear from you
Dick

August 25th
Dear Ed,

I enjoyed your August 18th letter. If you have short pieces written on all the topics you list, you need only some editing to have the bulk of a sizeable report. I can't really comment, of course, without seeing them, but they seem to indicate some creative and empirical thinking about the interplay of local and national actions over development issues. Have you looked back at some of the early ones, comparing them with later ones to see how your thinking has developed? Or to see how mutually consistent the early and later ones are?

Your comments about people getting killed by trains remind me of a paper I heard Ed Hoebel give on the "peaceful pueblos". He noted the high death rate by trains, but he was struck by the fact that the deaths were all of people who were heartily disliked, too aggressive, too dominant, opposed to the chiefs etc. His inference (and he backed it up by examples of traditional means of "disposing" surreptitiously of trouble makers) was that the "accidents" were ways of getting rid of problems. Though I would not suggest anything in your cases, the very fact of a high danger rate through accidents, suggests that no one would be too inquisitive should an engineered "accident" occur to someone who was generally disliked. If that avenue of social control really existed, there would be little incentive for anyone to go out on a limb and become too much of a leader, and one really ought to be prepared never to excite jealousy, as Hallowell suggested long ago.

What are the incentives to "improve things"? and the social controls on individualists?

All goes well here. The drought seems over with grey skies, while the furnace coming on over the weekend made Fall (and back to the regular grind of lectures) seem awfully imminent.

Good luck.

Dick

The Intellectual Mentor

The old adage about no one being an island is particularly relevant for scholarly pursuits. Who we are, in an intellectual sense, is the sum of those thinkers from the past who have moulded our thoughts and our academic contemporaries—students and professors. In my case, as it relates to the anthropological research in Collins, I now realize what an immense personal debt I owe to Richard Salisbury, my intellectual mentor. He originally came to McGill with an international reputation in the area of applied anthropology. As a student, Salisbury studied under the guidance of the distinguished S.F. Nadel at the Australian National University. Salisbury's book, *From Stone to Steel*, published on the basis of his fieldwork among the Saine in the New Guinea Highlands, was a landmark study which is still referred to in introductory texts today.

When Richard Salisbury came to McGill in 1971, he continued his emphasis on applied anthropology by invigorating the Anthropology of Development Programme, started by Norman Chance in the late 1960s. Before long, Salisbury had twenty or thirty M.A. and Ph.D. students under his auspices, most of whom he directed himself. Most of these students conducted original fieldwork among the James Bay Cree whose hunting lands were in danger of being flooded by the Provincial Government's hydro-electric project in northern Quebec.

Salisbury organized a weekly seminar in applied anthropology that was attended by several other McGill anthropologists, such as Carmen Lambert, Peter Sindel and Peter Gutkind. I remember attending presentations by Edmund Leach, Max Gluckman, Marvin Harris and Clifford Geertz, as well as other prominent anthropologists of the time. Through these gatherings, we kept up on each other's research and read each other's theses and papers, many of which were published by the Programme's "Brief Communication Series."

It was also evident that Salisbury's ideas, especially his emphasis on doing "useful" anthropology, were reflected in our own work. This view is further emphasized in the final lines of his book, *A Homeland for the Cree*, in which he proudly sums up:

> The Cree know that anthropologists vary: that some do better studies than others. They know that the knowledge that anthropologists

collect is useful knowledge—for all the work of the past decade [1971–1981] has been used by the Cree. (1986: 156)

When I returned to McGill after my period of fieldwork in northern Ontario, I felt that my own studies on political and economic change were of a similar nature to those conducted by others on "development" among the James Bay Cree. I could speak to the same issues, even though my work was quite far away in geographical terms. After my fieldwork in northern Ontario, I made a point of arranging a regular meeting time with Salisbury; we met for an hour a week for quite a few months. I remember feeling a bit guilty about this, because he always seemed quite busy when I went to see him. But he never turned me away. I realized that I had to take advantage of the opportunity of engaging in as many face-to-face discussions with him as I could, even though it meant being a bit "pushy."

Most of the time we talked about the specifics of my fieldwork, especially about how to translate everyday activities into generalized patterns, and then, into wider theoretical arguments. I got the impression that for Salisbury there was no such thing as a specific, isolated event. There are, rather, patterns and trends, inter-relationships and developments. We also talked about effective writing techniques. At first, I had a tendency to mix everything up: facts, analysis, and theory were mostly inseparable in my writing. I kept leaping about, through different levels of abstraction, which led to a fairly incoherent presentation. Salisbury took my work apart, separating these different facets. "Now," he would say, with all the pages scattered out before us, "in the beginning here, lay out your general theoretical approach—probing, asking questions, but not answering them. Suggest how your research in Collins could shed light on these issues. Then, go for quite a stretch presenting your facts and figures, the examples from your fieldwork. Leave the analysis to the end, then tie it up, suggesting answers to the problems that were posed in the beginning."

At other times Salisbury made a point of asking me about my own living situation—Was I comfortable with where I was living? Did I have a quiet place to work? How was the money situation working out? He also wanted to tell me about how the other students were doing—about problems they encountered in the field or about where they were going with their writing. There was no doubt that Salisbury kept directly in touch with all of us, socially and academically. For my part, my connection with Salisbury was extremely important. From my isolation in northern Ontario I felt connected to the intellectual environment at McGill and even further afield, to the general trends and issues in anthropology beyond Montreal.

Touchstones to Reality

The office of the Anthropology of Development Programme at McGill was situated at 3434 McTavish street in a renovated old stone house, suggesting an informal, family-like setting. As you climbed the narrow staircase to the second floor, you could hear the easy-going office chitchat. Liz, the secretary, was usually typing away. We would glance to the left to see if Salisbury was in his office. " Doc Salisbury," as we called him, was most often engaged in some animated conversation on the telephone. With his free hand, he would beckon us to come and take a seat. "Just another minute," Salisbury would whisper.

When I was back in Collins, I tried to keep this image in my mind, as a way of keeping touch with my ultimate purpose, which was to complete the fieldwork and get back to Montreal. When I received news from this office at McGill, I would seldom open the letter or package until I was safely hidden away in my cabin, my secure place of refuge. Contact with the people at McGill swallowed me up. I was transported away from the wood smoke, blackflies and everything else. I thought of such episodes as "touchstones to reality," but they were not really that at all. In fact, they were not much more than periods of idle escapism, although they had a purpose, because they reminded me about why I was in Collins in the first place. They helped to spring open the latches on the doors to the parts of my mind that were normally keep closed, so I could get on with life in Collins. Yet, day-dreaming can be a dangerous thing for an anthropologist. It is too easy to drift away to favourable climes and habitats where nothing presses upon us, where no demands are placed on our behaviour and where we feel secure, wanted and useful, the opposite, in fact, of the feelings of insecurity, disconnectedness and futility that can plague us during our fieldwork.

There is a line that anthropologists tread, in which we are partly in and partly out, disconnected on one side, connected on the other, seeing ourselves, seeing others. It is important that we be aware that we are on this line, just as it is important that we be aware of our own existence. It is like being a tightrope walker, someone who has to concentrate very carefully on the task at hand, yet at the same time try to do it unconsciously, so our instincts take over from our intellect. It is thinking which makes us what we are, but is also thinking that provides most of the traps that could destroy what we are trying to do in the first place.

There was a time when I dragged a heavy box back to my cabin. People at the Collins post office wanted to follow me to see what I had got, figuring, I imagine, that if they didn't receive anything, what would be the harm in them enjoying my mail? I resisted. No, this was my private space, in this box, it has to be explored by me alone, so that I can do my "touchstone with reality" trip, back to Montreal. The box was from a grad student friend of mine. He'd had field experience up in the Yukon, and so he knew how important these packages were. An "anthro's care package," I thought, as I pulled off the tape and string.

It was chock full of all sorts of things he knew I probably would be short of, could use in trade and so on. There were several cartons of cigarettes, bundles of assorted chocolate bars and magazines. No more nicotine fits. With the chocolate bars I could keep up with the trappers' hurried pace. Yes, Steve had been to the Yukon. Unfortunately, this was the last such box I was to receive.

I also used to occasionally get letters from a friend from Dundas, in southern Ontario. He was a fellow grad student at McMaster in my M.A. days. For some reason he addressed the letters to "Dr. Norval Norlander" or "Norval of the North." They were about hippie sort of things, like wind generators, Velokofsky's *Worlds in Collision* and other related, off-beat stuff. My mind wanders gently, as if buffeted by a soft, warm breeze off Collins Lake. Snap. Must get back to reality. What am I doing here? The big question that perpetually haunts me is: Will this demi-god called "culture shock" creep up on me, pounce and steal away my enterprise. And secondly: Is it necessary to keep such a vigilant guard?

There are psychological depths to the fieldwork enterprise that I feel are important to explore, but few have had much of a zest for getting into them. There has been only one explicit work that I know of, *Stress and Response in Fieldwork* (Henry and Saberwal 1969). We are reminded that the "ego-centred adjustment of the anthropologist to fieldwork" (ix) is a problem we should think about. The anthropologist comes in as a stranger and, if successful, leaves as a friend. This requires adjustments of a personal nature and the search for acceptance among the people who are participants in the study. We are also reminded of the anthropologists' need for flexibility. "Anthropologists who have worked in several field situations in depth find themselves accumulating separate social reference systems. Sometimes they even develop more that one social personality" (ix). Perhaps this is one of the reasons that anthropologists are expected to be a bit "loony" at times.

Most anthropologists I know have a curious mix of personal and social traits. They are outgoing and adventurous enough to interact with people in a variety of social and cultural settings. Yet, they also spend long hours in contemplative reflection, mulling over problems of kinship, social structure and the like. Some are able to continue this balancing act for most of their academic lives. Others, after the initial long-term field experience at the graduate level, revert to one side or the other. They either carry on one field project after another, never getting around to publishing the results, or they spend most of their lives "synthesizing" the ethnographies of others. Of course there are practical matters that come with establishing a career, raising a family, and so on, but some anthropologists find ways to navigate around these areas, systematically starting up another field project just as the manuscript for the last book is shipped off to the publisher. This suggests to me that the pitfalls really have a lot to do with our own limitations on the one hand and our drive to achieve excellence in our work on the other.

Pulling the Ideas Together

Thinking is every bit as important as writing, probably more so. Your field experiences first have to be conceptualized in some meaningful manner before they will make sense to anyone else. You have to think through the data, drawing it together around certain major and minor ideas. It was once suggested to me that I try to distill the whole field project down into a few lines or a paragraph. Salisbury, for example, once posed this question to me: "Can you see the entire fieldwork with that much clarity that a major purpose stands out above all else?"

In the beginning, of course, you force yourself to develop hypotheses about what you could expect in the fieldwork, based mostly on what others have done in the field. You try, in the beginning, to develop also a major point of departure from existing studies. This could entail filling in an ethnographic area that had been previously overlooked by researchers or it could involve a different interpretation of others' ethnographic studies. You go to the field to test ideas initially, but as time goes on and the flow of data that you are able to extract from the passage of everyday life starts to accumulate, you initiate new ideas on your own, ones less dependent on your original conceptualizations.

From my experience, the data collected in the field takes on a sort of family-tree diagram. The ideas are arranged in a hierarchical order, with the most important ones appearing near the top. As one travels downward through this diagram, it is as if the data and the interlinking ideas resemble family clusters or degrees of relatedness. In this way, the material begins to sort itself out into major themes, such as in my case into social, political and economic categories. Then, within each of these themes, further processes of organization and refinement can take place.

On Writing

The organizational component certainly facilitates putting your thoughts on paper. As Barrett has suggested: "a great deal of reflecting, planning, and organization must precede writing. My own approach is not to write a word of the actual manuscript until I have worked out the entire thing in my head" (1996: 232). In the end, though, people who are successful at writing develop their own style, work habits and "tricks of the trade" that work for them. It is largely a matter of experience and experimentation.

Here are a few of the things I have learned along the way, based on twenty-five years of writing anthropological material and this, my third book, on the subject. In the beginning of my career, I would just sit down and start with whatever came into my head, trying to be a bit chatty and interesting, the way a journalist might go about such work. I learned that this approach led to a lot of wasted effort. The problems were two-fold: I had neither an academically sound point nor a specific audience in mind. I obviously needed to revamp my approach to writing.

In my first publication based on the Collins fieldwork, I started by making three or four points that I thought would give the work academic or scholarly relevance. These points were linked together in a step-by-step process. For example, first, there was this problem in the literature dealing with patron-client relationships (that were discussed in the beginning of this book) having to do with an inattention to historical, cultural and environmental factors. Second, based on fieldwork among Collins' leaders, or patrons, these factors were important in conditioning the characteristics of local leadership patterns. I was thinking here of the traditional cultural background which encouraged generosity and a "sharing the wealth" ethic. Good hunters were expected to give freely the spoils of the hunt to others, especially those less fortunate or unable to adequately fend for themselves. This ethic, one could argue, was a social evolutionary adaptation that enhanced survival in a rugged and, at times, unforgiving, subarctic environment. Third, in a modern context, the ethic of generosity and sharing is seen to continue, as modern leaders distribute jobs, rather than game, to their followers. Fourth, the paper ends with a theoretical discussion on leadership and exchange theory suggesting that variations in patron-client relationships can be explained in large part by the environmental and cultural settings in which such relationships are embedded.

The approach, then, was to conduct a brief review of contemporary literature on a fairly narrowly defined topic, suggesting deficiencies or additions to this literature which would be used as a point of departure in establishing relevance for one's own work, a stretch of ethnographic reporting on details specific to the topic at hand and, finally, a discussion section which ties together theory, method, and ethnographic facts. Since this was my first attempt at publication, I chose a middle-range journal as my target. The journal, I reasoned, should have an editorial board with a process of refereed review. It should also have an interest in the subject matter of my paper, such as a concern for Aboriginal ethnography and the theoretical points raised in the papers. In the case of my patron-client paper, I ruled out journals dealing more specifically with aboriginal issues, such as *The Canadian Journal of Native Studies* because its audience was too diversified, which would require a much broader approach than the one I had taken. I also thought that it would be too premature to send it to one of the very big journals such as *American Anthropologist*, at least until I had much more expertise in my discipline. My choice in the end was a journal called *Man in the Northeast* (now titled *Northeastern Anthropology*), which agreed to publish my paper.

This initial publication was a great confidence booster, and so I set as my next goal the writing of a book based on the main themes outlined in the paper. The themes became chapters falling into the main areas of theoretical relevance—conditions and methods of fieldwork, kinship and social organization, economic pursuits and leadership patterns. Writing a book, I learned, was a lot different than writing a research paper. The much more extensive scope of the undertaking was a daunting task.

Writing forced me to work through several problems or barriers, most of which were of a personal nature. We all might recollect the cartoon image of a distraught writer who, after typing a few lines, pulls the paper out and discards it in the crumpled pile beside him. Many of us are perfectionist at heart. We want to do an exemplary job that will be remembered for some time. Maybe we think that this is the closest we will come to immortality. We are apt to put too much pressure on ourselves by thinking in such grandiose terms. This might well lead to the writer's greatest enemy—procrastination.

For many people, just getting started is the biggest challenge. They could be plagued with doubts. Will anybody like what I write? Will they think I'm stupid? What if I look like a fool? Each of us has to overcome issues such as these if we are to get on with the job. Here is what I tell myself: Most of us are lucky if anybody reads our material at all, so we should be grateful for that small blessing. Second, we are prone to insecurities because we attach too much self-importance to what we do. People are merely reading our writing; they are not passing judgement on who we are as a person. The fate of the world is not at stake here.

Successful people are able to set aside their egos for a while so that they can make their work better. They are able to make the best of criticism, to reflect for a moment on the pros and cons of what critics are saying about their work. Of course, we don't have to incorporate all suggestions for improvement, but there is usually a grain of truth in what is being said that we should think about. If we do not act defensively to suggestions, we stand a better chance of making our work much better than it was before. But believe me, it takes discipline to overcome these seemingly natural tendencies towards insecurity, self-protection and defensiveness.

The trick to it, I have learned, is to just get down to the job at hand, on as consistent a basis as we can. Nobody writes a book in just one day, so don't make the task of writing a monumental one. Books are written word by word, page by page, chapter by chapter. My students sometimes ask me "How do you write a book?" "I don't, really," is my answer. I explain that each day I just push the project forward a few pages. Some days are difficult, and on others, it all flows along like a breeze. But whatever the situation I don't stop pushing forward. I refuse to be stopped by "writer's block." "If you were able to write even three or four pages a day, on a consistent basis, week by week," I ask the students, "by the end of four or five months, how many pages would you have?" "That's eighty pages a month, or 320 pages in four months," as I quickly do the calculations for them. "These 320 pages probably would end up as well over 200 pages of print, which should be good enough, at least as a first draft. If you are consistent and don't strangle yourself by thinking too far ahead, the job is not as difficult as you might imagine it to be."

A routine of writing is important. Get yourself settled. If there is something bothering you, say in your personal life, try to set these issues aside. You don't want to constantly loose your concentration. Spend a few minutes, but not much more than ten or so, going over the end of the work that you did the day before. I read once that Earnest Hemmingway tried to end his writing for the day halfway through a thought or sentence and never at the end of a page, so that he could more readily pick up from where he had left off. I like to keep a notebook handy so that I can jot down ideas that keep cropping into my head while I'm writing. That way I can record them without having to concentrate on them for the time being. Later in the day, I'll go over them, to see if there's anything relevant that I can use. There is an unexpected thing that happens during the actual writing having to do with flashes of inspiration. Right out of the blue and quite unanticipated, we'll get a burst of perspective, a spurt of mental penetration, that allows us to make a significant leap forward in our work. It seems that as our consistency develops day-by-day in our writing, our mental activity just starts "cooking." Hitherto unforeseen insights emerge from a combination of all the other ideas that we have thrown into the cognitive mix of thought. It is important to keep track of these insights and to reflect on their different aspects and how they might contribute or fit into your work. They can be like nuggets of gold.

Consistency in writing for me develops out of an attempt to dissociate the composing part of my mental activity from any underlying fears and apprehensions that could trip me up. What this means is that I try to write at an even pace without much concern for the way that the words are actually coming out of my head. About the only editing that I do along the way is to change a few words here and there, if I'm being repetitive. I try to show no more concern for the actual process of writing that I would for how I'm walking. This reminds me of a quote from Max Weber in which he warns that methodology "can only bring us reflective understanding of the means which have demonstrated their value in practice by raising them to the level of explicit consciousness; it is no more the precondition of fruitful intellectual work than the knowledge of anatomy is the precondition for correct walking" (1949: 115). If we can condition ourselves to relax when we're writing, then we are less likely to have a cramping or paralysis of the mind take place. Relaxed mental activity allows for a greater chance of the emergence of serendipitous discovery in the way we interconnect various ideas.

The way to go about the writing process, for me in any event, is to try to hammer out that first draft as a manageable package without much concern for finesse or the niceties of composition. Later, when we have more time, we can do all the editing we want. We may need a lot of "bridging" pieces, made up of interconnecting paragraphs and pages, to give the work a more even flow. These may also be a need for more extensive introductory and concluding sections. I work on the idea that it doesn't hurt to repeat some of your main points several times, in key locations, as a method of getting the message across. It is a mistake to keep one's arguments too well hidden, for while we are very familiar with our work and what we are doing, most of the time readers will just make their way through it once. If only it were that easy for the writer.

As far as writing is concerned, most of us probably just whip ourselves to the task, and when we get down to it, the writing usually goes well. Many of us need little rituals to get started, like getting our coffee together, doing little exercises to loosen up our neck and shoulders or shuffling our papers. On this subject of rituals and getting started, Isaac Asimov apparently quipped, "Rituals? Ridiculous! My only ritual is to sit close enough to the typewriter so that my fingers touch the keys" (in Chiseri-Strater and Sunstein 1997: 279). And Asimov, one of my favourite writers, certainly had a way with words.

Chapter Eight

Conclusion:
Experience and Fieldwork

The unique qualitative aspects of a human existence that arise out of conditions of human experience ... must be thoroughly explored in all their ramifications and given more explicit formulation. —A. Irving Hallowell (1955: viii)

Leaving the field and going home is never an easy task for an anthropologist. Somehow you have managed to overcome all the difficulties that might have caused you to leave before the job was done. You have survived the psychological problems of culture shock and learned to cope with the long periods of isolation. There has been the stress of constant involvement in fieldwork, of never really being able to let go of what you are doing. You have become immersed in cultural activity foreign to your own—participated, observed, interviewed, taken notes and analyzed your data. But you have also made friends and now begin to think of this fieldwork community as your home. Just when you begin to think that you learned enough and feel comfortable enough to stay there forever, it is time to go, to return to the outside world that now seems in many respects as foreign to you as your fieldwork community did in the first place.

There is an interesting reversal to all of this. You arrive unsure of what you are doing; everything seems strange and difficult to cope with, the people look threatening and you are quite fearful about whether you can accomplish anything. Now, when you are about to leave, you feel "one of," many people tell you they do not want you to go. "Stay with us," they plead.

The city from where you once came now seems like the threatening environment. The people don't seem friendly here; how will you ever cope? The transition is not easy, in many ways going back seems more difficult than your first nights in your fieldwork community. There is an awakening to the thought that you must now face reality—no more fun and games, you must get on with your life. There are reports to be written, money to be earned, jobs to be sought after. Back in your fieldwork community, you were somebody; here, in the city, you are just another anonymous face in the crowd.

When I thought back to my life in Collins, I could picture the people laughing and joking with one another, seemingly without any cares. I missed this carefree life, where you knew who you were and where you stood in the community. But I didn't harbour any romantic notions about life in the northern bush. Life wasn't easy there. I learned from firsthand experience about the people's hunger, the anxieties of not being able to adequately clothe their children and the cabins burning down because of rotten stoves. Many young people, especially the teenaged mothers, seemed old beyond their years.

Through it all, I developed an appreciation for life no matter where you live. There are joys in life, despite the hardships that come along. There are good and bad people everywhere. You just have to learn about the difference between individuals, about the qualities that make them who they are. Of course you have to learn about yourself too. Inevitably, if I were to make a success of fieldwork, I would have to find out who I was, what I was capable of and what were the levels of my own incompetence.

Anthropologists often say that their fieldwork changed them, and while it may sound a bit trite, it is true in my case. It's as if fieldwork makes an indelible impression on your psyche, altering forever the way you view the people, places and things of this world. Partly, I feel, this is because the fieldwork experience is so intense—you have to concentrate on what's going on around you twenty-four hours a day, forcing yourself into a hyper sense of awareness. You are constantly forcing tidbits of information into your memory, much more so than you would do in normal life, and it becomes difficult to release this stuff at some later date. I explained at the outset that one of the reasons for writing this book was to provide some measure of closure on that part of my life. The idea was that recording these events might allow me to let go of this fieldwork stuff that for so many years I have been reluctantly carrying around in my head. Maybe other anthropologists don't have this sort of trouble after fieldwork; it's hard to say, we don't talk about it much, and I'm not aware of anyone who has written about this problem of "fieldwork closure" in more than a cursory manner.

As we near the end of this book, it would be useful to sort through some of the central issues that have been discussed thus far, as a means of tying them together. The discussion throughout these chapters can be seen to operate at two different levels. At the level of concrete details, this work has tried to explore various facets of the fieldwork experience in social/cultural anthropology—the rational for beginning a study, the situations, events and personalities that are the "stuff" of living in a community, leaving and writing up. At another, more general level is a wider theoretical discussion carried on about the intrinsic nature of ethnography or qualitative research.

Ethnography and Epistemology

The central point made in this book is that the main epistemological (knowledge creation) issues in anthropology are intrinsically tied to fieldwork. Since anthropologists gather information on their subjects of interest mainly on the basis of first-hand field research, then the inter-relationship between fieldwork and the creation of knowledge in anthropology is a matter of deep interest.

Certainly one of the main lessons that ethnographic research has for anthropology is that the search for general statements of the structure of knowledge may be precluded by the very facts of cultural variation. There would appear to be few cross-cultural generalizations that can be made concerning such things as proper conduct, morality and, ultimately, truth.

There is then an epistemological dilemma or contradiction in the task of anthropology. If our concern is with epistemology as the theory of knowledge, with the pursuit of basic questions concerning the search for truth, then we might have to be prepared for the development of a "culturally embedded" methodology that would be capable of dealing with the sorts of variations in points of view, in accepted traditions and "truths" that anthropologists have to deal with. What this all suggests is that there is some validity to Peter Winch's argument that it is not empirical verification that confirms what is in agreement with reality, but rather it is intersubjective communicative competence that constitutes reality in each social matrix. As he explains, "A man's [sic] social relations with his fellows are permeated with his ideas about reality. Indeed, `permeated' is hardly a strong enough word: social relations are expressions of ideas about reality" (1958: 23).

Thus, we are confronted again with this question about "reality," and how it is understood in culturally defined contexts. In the process we are also led back to the essential role of fieldwork, since it conditions the anthropologist's worldview in a general sense. What emerges from this view is an appreciation, even an affection, for the diversity of human cultures around the world— Geertz's "great (and wasting) resource." In other words, this philosophical bent to my discussion is really all about the biggest of questions for anthropology, which, to allow Geertz to phrase it: "The great natural variation of cultural forms is, of course, not only anthropology's great (and wasting) resource, but the ground for its deepest theoretical dilemma: how is such variation to be squared with the biological unity of the human species" (1973: 22)? The fundamental epistemological problem in anthropology is therefore the simultaneous notions of cultural uniqueness and the underlying similarity of *homo sapiens*.

Yet, there are no doubt anthropologists who feel that this "deepest theoretical dilemma" cannot be resolved unless they move beyond the "immediacy of local detail" that one encounters in fieldwork situations. For it is fieldwork that is primarily responsible for the anthropological emphasis on the uniqueness of human cultures and for the relativistic view that each human culture views the world on its own terms. It follows then that fieldwork poses certain epistemological problems for anthropology about how knowledge in a general sense is to be studied. It also follows that a central problem in anthropology is that fieldwork could induce us into the mistaken belief that all knowledge is relative, or even further, that reliable knowledge is not possible.

It is fieldwork which nonetheless poses broad, comparative questions, even when new orthodoxies tell us they are obsolete. It is fieldwork which brings surprises, such a ghosts in a northern Ontario cabin. My fieldwork encounter with the Ojibwa man in my cabin or our discussion about whether or not I was aware of Ed Pigeon's ghost near my stove was a problem because I did not initially come to the community to study ghosts, religion or other such phenomena. My central concern at the time was with politics, leadership and economic development, so I did not pay any particular attention to what the man was talking about. When I began to reflect on my fieldwork experiences, this ghost episode would creep into my consciousness. When it did so, I was belatedly forced to ponder some very fundamental issues concerning my fieldwork experience, such as: To what extent did our concepts of "ghost" coincide, if at all? What "message" was he actually trying to communicate to me concerning the ghost phenomenon?

Later in my fieldwork, I began to realize that the man was not just posing a question about whether or not I was able to see the ghost, but that he was actually "seeing" it and wanted me to be party in some way to this experience. I began to realize, in ways that were not immediately obvious to me in the initial stages of my fieldwork, that the Ojibwa people took the existence of "ghosts" as pretty much a routine matter, like dogs, trees and so on. For them it was sort of belabouring the obvious to have to point out to the anthropologist the existence of ghosts in his cabin. Over the years this experience haunted me (no pun intended)—a piece of fieldwork flotsam that was not part of my research plan. The issues raised were of comparative epistemology—the translation of *cheebuy* as "ghost," the Ojibwa belief in and experience of *cheebuy*, and the rationality or irrationality of the "knowledge" of such phenomena.

Since the question of evidence is also central to the pursuit of epistemology, we are thus confronted with the challenges that our sources of knowledge bring to us from the fieldwork experience. All debates and controversies are ultimately reducible to the epistemological question: "How do we know what we know?" From the anthropological perspective, there does not appear to exist any one single interpretation of phenomena that is any more valid or real than any other. I conclude that the relative nature of the human experience means that the means of proving the existence of an objective reality is a problem without a readily available solution. The argument stemming from the discussion and analysis of examples in this book is that anthropologists should refocus their epistemological questions in the discipline to issues related to the role of ethnographers' experiences in fieldwork. It is this focus on personal experiences, I argue, that will allow for the greatest possibility for understanding the manner in which ethnography is actually created. Thus, it makes considerable sense for contemporary anthropologists to explore the meaning of experience, its epistemological status and its place in fieldwork.

Experience and Fieldwork

The conventional view of anthropology is that the fieldworker travels to an exotic place, usually somewhere quite different from his home environment, and assumes the role of a stranger. This stranger-position is well-documented in the literature, such as Powdermaker's *Stranger and Friend* (1966), Nash's "The Ethnologist as Stranger" (1963) and Agar's *The Professional Stranger* (1980).

The role of stranger has its obvious disadvantages. One is apt to know little about the customary modes of behaviour among the local people. It would be very easy under such circumstances to unknowingly violate acceptable rules of behaviour. One has to contend with strange foods, housing and sanitary conditions, everyday greeting conventions and establishing rapport. Added to these concerns are "Problems of getting started, of establishing a routine of living and a pattern of systematic work, and of functioning within the indigenous power structure.... Discouragements and becoming fed-up ... to tensions and anxieties (Powdermaker 1966: 14). Beyond this, as Nash (1963) indicates, the ethnographer not only faces extreme adaptive problems in the field, there is the additional scholarly or research pressure of collecting fairly complete data on a culture within a very limited period of time. Few other strangers are so dependent upon making successful adjustments. It is no wonder that many ethnographers feel that they are working under a "do or die" or "sink or swim" atmosphere in their fieldwork.

The stranger role, though, also has its advantages. This is what Barrett refers to as "stranger value," "that is, people would confide in the foreign anthropologist and reveal information that they would conceal from indigenous scholars" (1996: 25). In my own experience in Collins, numerous people confided personal information to me. They could unburden themselves of some problems they were unable to share with others in the community because they were afraid that it would be spread around as gossip. A fieldworker is often regarded as a good listener, someone who is genuinely interested in their concerns. Being a stranger also means that one will likely be approached in the initial stages of the fieldwork by certain people that Agar refers to as "stranger-handlers." As he explains, "Most groups have official or unofficial stranger-handlers to deal with outsiders. Such stranger-handlers are natural public relations experts. They can find out what the outsider is after and quickly improvise some information that satisfies him without representing anything potentially harmful to the groups" (Agar 1980: 85).

In Collins, Peter and Donald were the community's "stranger-handlers." Everyone who came to the village, especially anyone of any importance, would first meet these two brothers. They would take you to their home, provide a meal or two for you, and maybe set you up with accommodations. Ultimately, though, they were primarily interested in finding out what your business was for being in Collins. Some outsiders, such as government officials and religious personnel, had rather obvious and straightforward reasons.

There were others, such as the anthropologist, who posed a potential problem.

I know in my own case that Peter and Donald were quite curious about what I was up to but were nonetheless guarded for a long period of time. There was a feeling-out process involved, as they asked me many questions about what information I wanted to collect, who would read it, and how the people and the village would be portrayed. There was certainly a lot of "impression management" going on here. Many of their questions hinted at an apprehension that I would find out and reveal Collins peoples' "dark and hidden" secrets. In this way I might be regarded as a threat. I would eventually find out, as I penetrated further with my questioning, information that no normal outsider would ever hope to learn. There were such things as mysterious deaths, marital affairs, abusive relationships, incestuous episodes, and the like. People didn't want me finding out about the happenings in this "inner stage," to use Goffman's term.

The people know that it is unavoidable that the anthropologist will eventually discover many of these secrets if he or she stays in the community long enough. This is where rapport and trust come in. I went to great lengths to explain to people that I did have a specific research agenda for my research. This meant collecting information primarily on political and economic matters, but that the wider context of community relationships, such as their family and kinship patterns, were also important to me. My field notes would be safeguarded from prying eyes, I explained, and the information gathered would only be used for "scientific purposes," by which I meant, to test certain theoretical issues in anthropology. In a further attempt to allay their fears, I tried to reassure them that I would exercise a certain amount of discrimination in how the information would we disseminated. In the beginning, I referred to Collins as "Wolf River." Later, however, the people indicated that they were proud of their attempts to build their tourist lodge at Whitewater Lake and that it would be all right to use the name of Collins in my publications.

When my first book, *The Ogoki River Guides*, was to be published, I made a special trip back to Collins with a draft of the manuscript. I went over this with people, allowing them to read what was being said about them and to make comments or corrections as they saw fit. Some people did not like what was written about them, especially if it portrayed them in a less than favourable light. Donald, for example, did not like me to reveal that his local nickname was *monskish*, or "moose-nose."

This nickname was an apt one, I thought, because it conveys a sense of his brashness, like a moose crashing through the bush, apparently oblivious to the noise created. Donald certainly "called them as he saw them," whether you liked it or not. Actually, I saw this characteristic as an immense to help to the Collins political environment, especially when it came to dealing with government officials. Donald had no qualms about getting on the phone and calling Queen's Park in Toronto, demanding to speak to a deputy minister. He would get his way more times than not over some problem with funding for the tourist lodge or anything else that was on his mind. It is totally inconceivable to me that anyone else in Collins would dare to be so brash and straightforward.

When it came to reviewing the manuscript, Donald would search through the pages looking for any reference to himself, scrutinizing it closely. He would act hurt, irritated or feign some other emotional response in an attempt to have me change what I had written. I explained, "Donald, I'm only interested in accuracy here. If you feel something that I've written is wrong, or not correctly portrayed, then tell me, but otherwise nobody is going to believe a word of this if you come across as God's gift to mankind. We all have our foibles and idiosyncrasies—it's what makes us human."

Peter's approach was entirely different. He would just laugh at what I had written about Donald. "Don't change a word," he would insist. "This is what makes the book interesting. Donald is sulking now, but he'll get over it." Peter's approach was more intellectual in nature. He wanted me to explain to him the theoretical argument that I was pushing; he wanted the bigger picture on what I was doing in Collins. Peter grasped that the research on Collins was mainly for illustrative purposes, that there was a larger plan in operation here having to do with economic development and political change. These discussion with Peter were of immense help to me in solidifying my own academic position. He would point out inconsistencies to me or add additional information from the Collins case that I was not aware of. Having Peter as an informant, friend and confidant was an enormous benefit to me in so many ways; every other fieldworker should be so fortunate.

Crossing Boundaries

I went to Collins as a stranger and left with some life-long friends. In the process of making these friends, my fieldwork involved crossing certain boundaries that were partly cultural and partly personal. Dealing with boundaries is the stock in trade of the ethnologist. You must learn to live in strange and unusual conditions, eat different foods, possibly learn another language, and find out how to interact with people on their own cultural terms and how to develop a degree of rapport with them so that they will be trusting enough to give you information and allow you to participate in their activities.

The fieldworker learns to do all of these things, not through courses and guidebooks, but through a trial and error process of experience. The old adage about experience being the best teacher certainly applies to the adaptive process that ethnographers must go through to be successful in their work. But what of the personal boundaries? As people, we bring with us to the field certain personal strengths and weaknesses. Some of us have a lot of difficulty in overcoming inhibitions that prevent us from becoming effective fieldworkers. It is difficult for most of us to be open and friendly with strangers, especially in cultural settings much different from what we are used to. This is especially true if developing rapport becomes difficult or if people rebuff our information gathering initiatives. Many fieldworkers probably spend some time "hiding out" from people, as they begin to crave more private space. Isolating from the community at large for short periods of time can have salubrious effects if it allows us time to reflect and organize our field material. It can also allow us to rest up or re-group our energies so that later we can begin again, refreshed with renewed vigour. It is not such a good thing if isolation turns to withdrawal and avoidance. For most researchers, over-identification is not the problem. What is difficult about fieldwork is the constant pressure to stay tuned into what is happening in a community. It is a challenge to live an ever-present role of involvement. Some get fed up and leave, without completing their research objectives; others seem to excel under the pressure.

This challenge of completing a research project in anthropology forces us to confront our own strengths and weakness, to learn about who we are as people and to find out what we are capable of and what we are not. There is no doubt that fieldwork is a personal journey as much as it is an academic or intellectual one. It is in this personal sense that one might make a case for anthropology not being a science in the conventional use of the term. "Unlike the natural sciences," Barrett says, "the social sciences are subjective, and the observer or researcher has an impact on his or her research" (1996:31). Powdermaker (1966) also points to this aspect of fieldwork that involves a continuing relation between personal feelings and intellectual perception. Fieldwork is made up of what the researcher feels as well as what he or she actually does, since the anthropologist is part of the situation studied.

"In recounting my field experiences," Powdermaker explains, "I look forward as well as outward, with the benefit of hindsight. An anthropological voyage may tack and turn in several directions, and the effective field worker learns about himself as well as about the people he studies" (1966: 14). In my own case, there were many times that I had to force myself out of my little cabin, to join in and become part of. This was especially true in the winter months, when the sun began setting about 4:30 p.m. and darkness enveloped our little world in the bush. At times the world seemed to be closing in on me, and in a strange sort of way, I began to like the isolation and solitude. I'd tune into the radio, listening to stations in Chicago, Fort Wayne or Dallas. My mind drifted away to these places; away from the ever-beckoning call of fieldwork.

More times than not, it wasn't very long before someone paid me a visit. Usually they just said they were passing by and asked if I needed something from the store. Looking back, I realize that the people must have cared about me or they wouldn't have bothered checking, although I didn't think this at the time. Actually, I thought of myself as bothering them too much, although most people put up with all my questions with a joking good humour. I wonder what I would have been like if they were asking all the questions—would I have become grumpy, peevish or difficult to get along with? They usually didn't, although I fear I might well have under the circumstances.

It makes you wonder at times why anyone should be interested in becoming involved in all this boundary crossing, especially with the difficulties involved. However, in my case, my growing up years in Beardmore were probably not a whole lot different from how northern Native boys and girls grow up, despite some of the other cultural differences. When I went to Collins, I was already accustomed to life in the bush and with what one had to do to survive there. What were the implications of these personal experiences of mine for my later fieldwork? For one thing, I certainly felt that I was much less of a "stranger" to the people than would normally have been the case for a "southerner." On the material or technological side of life, there was not that much difference between their lifestyle and the one that I was familiar with from my childhood. On the other hand, I couldn't rightly say that I was an "insider" either. My cultural tradition, Euro-Canadian, was much different. Living in Collins, in the Ojibwa people's own element, I would come to learn that they thought about the world in much different terms than I did. The traditional bush lore and the spiritual creatures were in stark contrast to my Roman Catholic upbringing. Other important differences that I learned about later were the organization of families, the modes of expression in their Ojibwa language and their manner of interaction in interpersonal relationships.

My personal background made me "partly in and partly out" of the fieldwork in which I would eventually become immersed. This background provided me with definite advantages in the field. This was especially true in the day-to-day aspects of living in Collins, such as coping with the cold and the snow and eating a bush diet of fish, moose and beaver meat, as well as carrying water, chopping wood, ice-fishing, wearing snowshoes, fixing an oil stove, reading with a coal oil lamp, breaking trail, living in a log cabin or cleaning fish.

If there were any drawbacks to my upbringing as a child, it was that these activities, which would be largely foreign to the city dweller, were familiar to me. Seeing an old fellow sitting in the sun stringing a pair of snowshoes might have fascinated someone else—I certainly didn't think to make a lot of drawings or diagrams about how one went about this sort of work. The unfortunate part of my background was that it served to partially blind me to what I perceived as the common or banal aspects of northern bush life.

As a consequence, I tended to focus my fieldwork on those aspects of life that I found different from what I was used to. I was fascinated with the social organizational aspects of northern Native life and concentrated much of my intellectual effort in attempts to understand the various facets of kinship, family life, band organization and so on. The way Ojibwa social life was patterned was so different from my own understanding of "culture and society" that I developed an intense curiosity for the various nuances of social life, such as the names they used to address each other, their social patterns of interaction and their little quirks, like women quickly putting a hand over their mouths when they were embarrassed or wanted to say something "under their breath."

There is a double-edged methodological issue here having to do with cultural boundaries. If the locale of our research is one that we are already quite conversant with, then we run the risk of overlooking that which is familiar. The advantages, though, are that we can "set up shop" rather quickly, expending less effort and time securing our food and accommodations. Rapport with the people could be a less difficult task as well, if we are in tune with their problems, social, economic or otherwise.

When research is conducted in a cultural setting that is very exotic or far removed from our own, then we are apt to spend an inordinate amount of time just foraging to keep alive. Rapport with the local population, because of linguistic and cultural barriers, could take many months to establish, if it happens at all. In years past, one could hire servants and informants, although I suspect that this is not common practice today. Powdermaker, for example, in her fieldwork in the Melanesian island of Lesu in 1929–1930 informs us that "Servants are a necessity in field situations where living conditions are primitive. Wood has to be chopped, birds and game shot, water carried from a distance, cooking done over an open fire, clothes washed on rocks and ironed with a charcoal iron, and other chores done in an equally primitive way" (1966: 69).

My own living conditions in Collins would appear to have been just about as "primitive." There are certain activities in the field that you do not try to duplicate, though, from your home environment. It's hard to imagine the necessity of ironing your clothes when those around you might not even wash theirs for weeks. For the sake of convenience, I let things go when I had to. Bathing was done with the aid of a wash basin or as a swim in the lake during the warmer months. While I had an edge in coping with living conditions in the northern bush, I also felt that I could reduce the distance between myself and the local people if I tried to do things the way they did. It was all part of the "participation" side of fieldwork. When I was outside cleaning a fish or partridge for my supper, people would drop by to chat for a while, offering the odd hint on how to do the job more effectively. These little conversations provided invaluable insights at times into people's thinking and attitudes. Under these conditions, hiring a servant would have seemed outlandish, suggesting also that I was aloof and unapproachable. In other words, the fieldworker has to be aware of the cultural boundary and develop some sort of practical strategy for coping with it.

This methodological problem of crossing borders and boundaries, according to Stephenson (1993), is an "issue of practicality" and perspective. For illustrative purposes Stephenson quotes a Jewish observer of the German army marching into Paris in 1940 who notes, rather perversely, "This is a great day for the people of Indochina." Stephenson's point is that "it matters rather a lot who is crossing just what border. Too abstract or universal a notion of borders will, I fear, risk a unidimensional understanding by privileging the notion of borders over the people who cross them... a parallax perspective [is] one where objects appear to change position when observed from different points (1993:

59). The possible liberation of Indochina from French occupation, coincident with the Nazi occupation of France, would indicate that border crossings have an ironic element to them. And, as Johannes Fabian (1993) notes, border crossings involve acts of "submission"—"the border [is] a place and time of dominance/submission." The image evoked by Fabian is that of boundary crossings as matters of control and power.

These are certainly issues to which anthropologists should pay attention. The globalization of culture means the dissolution of some boundaries, such as those surrounding the modern nation-state, at a time when others are in the process of consolidation, e.g., in the arenas of class, gender and the political economy of powers. Anthropology's view of local cultures as essentially time-less, bounded and self-contained has become obsolete. A new set of images—of flux, motion and variability of interpretation—is in vogue. The demise of traditional boundaries has blurred the edges of anthropology, with the prolifera-tion of "cultural studies" and the sharing of this territory with literary critics, historians and others. This is not to say that such boundary transgressions in academic disciplines cannot lead to mutually enriching experiences. However, as Roger Keesing warns: "My only concern about all this crossing of disciplinary boundaries is that the fences cultural anthropologists are jumping nowadays lead us into the even squishier turf of the humanities. Few of us are jumping fences into more solid terrain" (1993: 58).

What is this elusive "solid terrain" of which Keesing speaks, and what of the future of anthropology? Is anthropology headed for "its own liquidation," as Fabian (1991: 262) predicts? It may be that differences in the worlds of thought and experience, as portrayed by past generations of fieldworkers, were over-stated. But this is largely a matter of theoretical debate, to be resolved in the domain of fieldwork. Bringing fieldwork issues closer to, not farther from, the realm of theoretical debate would appear the most productive way of ensuring anthropology's future.

Review of Issues

There is an old saying about conclusions to the effect that there are no real endings, just new beginnings. Of course it all depends I suppose on which end of the spectrum of change you view this from. The caterpillar undergoing metamorphosis may be quite concerned about the death of its old self, unaware of an emergence as a beautiful butterfly. The relevance of this observation about butterflies is that my initial intention in writing this book was to provide some sort of closure on my old anthropological life. I wanted to reflect on my fieldwork experiences in Nipigon country, to put things on paper for safekeep-ing, so that I didn't carry them around in my head anymore. This was an attempt to move on to something new. Here are a few of the things I discovered in the thinking and writing process of this book from the beginning until now.

First, if I hadn't forced myself to reflect on my fieldwork experiences and to commit them to paper, I probably wouldn't have had the opportunity to rethink, in-depth, on the wider significance of the events, people and circumstances that formed the fieldwork experience. I don't mean here the theoretical issues about patron-client relations, economic development and the like that were important at the time. These I have already written about quite extensively. Rather, I am thinking about the wider meaning of fieldwork, or qualitative research, in and of itself, and of the impact that such experiences have on one's life.

Going to the field involves many unknowns, despite our well-thought-out methodological plans and theoretical designs. We don't know about the people we will meet, the situations we will encounter or even if we will be capable of carrying out the task at all. As we go along, from day to day and month to month, we try our best to muddle through and to keep up with what is going on. We are disappointed that some people don't seem to particularly care for us, and we are grateful for the people we get along with on especially good terms. There will be regrets about things we did or maybe didn't do.

At a second level, there is this business of the meaning of experience and its place in fieldwork. Surprisingly little has been written on this subject, especially in a direct, explicit sense. Perhaps it has just been taken for granted— we all have experiences in the field, but so what? I suspect that this lack of reflection on experience has had to do with a mind-set that keeps the ethnographer safely hidden in the background, emerging only rarely to interject the odd personal comment or two. The real focus is on the so-called "objective reality" of concrete facts and figures. In other words, a decidedly positivistic bent to one's approach to fieldwork would not suggest a necessity to reflect on the ethnographer's role, the subjective nature of interpretation or the various possible vantage points that could be taken in any given fieldwork situation. I argue that reflection on what is going on, both personally and academically, is a great advantage in conducting fieldwork. Ethnographers are not insensitive robots; we feel, and this has a bearing on such matters as empathy with informants and participation in the community. We also need a perspective on how our own behaviour has an impact on the "objects" of our study, as well as on our own research. Fieldwork is a subjective experience, and the influences on the research go both ways—the people in a community are affected by our presence and involvement in their affairs, and, in turn, they influence the ongoing nature of fieldwork both at theoretical and personal levels.

Fieldwork is the bedrock of the anthropological enterprise. It is the forum in which our debates are decided; the final arbiter in our disputes. The definitive problem of anthropology is to confront the challenge concerning the fieldwork experience and the sorts of knowledge that derive from this activity. All of our controversies and debates are reducible in the end to the epistemological question about our sources of information and about how it is that we come to know what we do. If you adhere to the philosophical perspective of cultural relativism, then there does not appear to exist any one interpretation of human behaviour that is any more valid than any other. It's all largely a matter of perspective. This relativistic nature of the human experience makes the existence of an objective reality a highly problematic issue; one, I would think, that lacks a readily available solution, even as we strive to predict and to explain. It is unlikely that any "laws" of human behaviour or cultural phenomena will be discovered in the future. We should be concentrating on "experience" in fieldwork as an essential facet of the knowledge gathering process in anthropology. We could learn much more about fieldwork if we were to concentrate efforts on elaborating the meaning of experience and its epistemological status in ethnography.

Conclusion

This book has been about lessons learned and about how one might profit from the personal experiences gained during the course of ethnographic research. Socrates' off-quoted sentiment that the unexamined life is not worth living resonates with Hallowell's suggestion that "the conditions of human experience ... must be thoroughly explored in all their ramifications" (1955: viii). When it comes to fieldwork, it is this sort of exploratory work that has the potential to greatly enhance knowledge about ourselves, about the informants who are pivotal to our studies and about the essential merits of anthropology as a whole.

Anthropologists have opportunities today for change and growth, based on the traditional strengths of their discipline. There is also an opportunity here to reaffirm the enduring merits of the discipline, based on learning through observation and participation, and thereby provide a more solid foundation for future advances. After all, it is long-term fieldwork that is primarily responsible for the contributions that anthropology has made to our knowledge of humanity. It has been fieldwork that has carried us this far, from the days of Boas and Malinowski, and which will provide the platform for whatever advances anthropology is capable of launching in this new millennium.

References

Abu-Lughod, L. 1991. "Writing Against Culture." In R.G. Fox (ed.), *Recapturing Anthropology*. Sante Fe, NM: School of American Research Press.

Agar, M.H. 1980. *The Professional Stranger: An Informal Introduction to Ethnography*. San Diego: Academic Press.

Asad, T. (ed.). 1973. *Anthropology and the Colonial Encounter*. Atlantic Highlands, NJ: Humanities Press.

Barak, V. 1988. "Review of: G.E. Marcus and M.J. Fischer, Anthropology as Cultural Critique." *Culture* 8 (2): 100–101.

Barrett, S.R. 1976. "The Use of Models in Anthropological Fieldwork." *Journal of Anthropological Research* 32: 161–81.

_____. 1979. "Social Anthropologist: Marginal Academic?" *Canadian Review of Sociology and Anthropology* 16: 367–86.

_____. 1988. *The Rebirth of Anthropological Theory*. University of Toronto Press.

_____. 1996. *Anthropology: A Student's Guide To Theory and Method*. University of Toronto Press.

_____. 1998a. "Review of: Thomas A. Dunk, It's a Working Man's Town." *Anthropologica* XL: 146.

_____. 1998b. "Forcasting Theory: Problems and Exemplars in the Twenty-First Century." Paper presented at the 14th International Congress of Anthropological and Ethnological Sciences, July 26–August 1.

Boldt, M. 1993. *Surviving as Indians*. University of Toronto Press.

Briggs, Jean. 1970. *Never in Anger*. Cambridge: Harvard University Press.

Carrithers, M. 1990. "Is Anthropology Art or Science?" *Current Anthropology* 31 (3): 263–82.

Chiseri-Strater, E., and B. S. Sunstein. 1997. *FieldWorking: Reading and Writing Culture*. Upper Saddle River, NJ: Prentice-Hall.

Clifford, J., and G. Marcus (eds.). 1986. *Writing Culture: The Poetics and Politics of Ethnography*. Berkeley: University of California Press.

DeVita, P.R. (ed.). 1992. *The Naked Anthropologist: Tales from Around the World*. Belmont, CA: Wadsworth.

Dickason, O.P. 1993. *Canada's First Nations*. Toronto: McClelland and Stewart.

Dunning, R.W. 1959. *Social and Economic Change Among the Northern Ojibwa*. University of Toronto Press.

Dyck, N. 1990. "Cultures, Communities and Claims: Anthropology and Native Studies in Canada." *Canadian Ethnic Studies* 22 (3): 40–55.

Fabian, J. 1991. *Time and Work of Anthropology*. Reading: Harwood Academic Publishers.

_____. 1993. "Crossing and Patrolling: Thoughts on Anthropology and Boundaries." *Culture* XIII (1): 49–54.

Fischer, John L. 1958. "The Classification of Residence in Censuses." *American*

Anthropologist 60: 508–17.

Frideres, J.S. 1993. *Native Peoples in Canada*. Scarborough, ON: Prentice Hall.

Geertz, C. 1973. *The Interpretation of Cultures*. New York: Basic Books.

_____. 1983. *Local Knowledge: Further Essays in Interpretive Anthropology*. New York: Basic Books.

_____. 1990. "Comment: Is Anthropology Art or Science?" *Current Anthropology* 31 (3): 274.

Goodenough, W. 1956. "Residence Rules." *Southwestern Journal of Anthropology* 12: 22–37.

Gutkind, P.C.W. 1969. "The Social Researcher in the Context of African National Development: Reflections of an Encounter." In F. Henry and S. Saberwal (eds.), *Stress and Response in Fieldwork*. New York: Holt, Rinehart and Winston.

Hallowell, A.I. 1955. *Culture and Experience*. Philadelphia: University of Pennsylvania Press.

_____. 1992. *The Ojibwa of Berens River, Manitoba*. New York: Holt, Rinehart and Winston.

Hayano, D.M. 1990. *Road Through the Rain Forest: Living Anthropology in Highland Papua New Guinea*. Prospect Heights, IL: Waveland Press.

Hedican, E.J. 1982a. "The Whitesand Ojibwa: Land Claims and the Societal Mediator." In C. Geisler et al. (eds.), *Indian SIA: The Social Impact Assessment of Rapid Resource Development on Native Peoples*. Ann Arbor: University of Michigan Press.

_____. 1982b. "Governmental Indian Policy, Administration, and Economic Planning in the Eastern Subarctic." *Culture* 2 (3): 25–36.

_____. 1985. "Modern Economic Trends Among the Northern Ojibwa." *Man in the Northeast* 30: 1–25.

_____. 1986a. *The Ogoki River Guides: Emergent Leadership among the Northern Ojibwa*. Waterloo: Wilfrid Laurier University Press.

_____. 1986b. "Anthropologists and Social Involvement: Some Issues and Problems." *The Canadian Review of Sociology and Anthropology* 23 (4): 544–58.

_____. 1987. "The Land Base Problem among Canadian Native People." *The Rural Sociologist* 7 (5): 459–64.

_____. 1990a. "The Economics of Northern Native Food Production." In J.I. (Hans) Bakker (ed.), *The World Food Crisis: Food security in Comparative Perspective*. Toronto: Canadian Scholar's Press.

_____. 1990b. "Richard Salisbury's Anthropology: A Personal Account." *Culture* 10 (1): 14–18.

_____. 1990c. "On the Rail-Line in Northwestern Ontario: Non-Reserve Housing and Community Change." *The Canadian Journal of Native Studies* 10 (1): 15–32.

_____. 1991. "On the Ethno-Politics of Canadian Native Leadership and Identity." *Ethnic Groups* 9 (1): 1–15.

_____. 1994. "Epistemological Implications of Anthropological Fieldwork, with Notes from Northern Ontario." *Anthropologica* 36: 205–24.

_____. 1995. *Applied Anthropology in Canada: Understanding Aboriginal Issues*. University of Toronto Press.

_____. 1999. "Aboriginal Cultural Revival in Canada: Resistance and Change." Paper presented to the Second Regional Conference on Social Movements and Change, International Sociological Association, University College Cork, Ireland, 16–18th April.

Heggenhoughen, K. 1992. "The Inseparability of Reason and Emotion in the Anthropological Perspective: Perceptions upon Leaving 'The Field.'" In P.R. DeVita (ed.), *The Naked Anthropologist: Tales From Around the World*. Belmont, CA: Wadsworth Publishing.

Henry, F. 1966. "The Role of the Fieldworker in an Explosive Political Situation." *Current Anthropology* 7: 552–59.

Henry, F., and S. Saberwal (eds.). 1969. *Stress and Response in Fieldwork*. New York: Holt, Rinehart and Winston.

Huxley, Aldous. 1932. *Texts and Pretexts*. London: Chatto and Windus.

Kaplan, A. 1964. *The Conduct of Inquiry*. San Francisco: Chandler Publishing.

Keesing, Roger M. 1993. "The Lens of Enchantment." *Culture* XIII (1): 57–59).

Kluckhohn, Clyde. 1957. *Mirror for Men*. New York: Fawcett World Library.

Landes, Ruth. 1937a. *Ojibwa Sociology*. New York: Columbia University Press.

_____. 1937b. "The Ojibwa of Canada." In M. Mead (ed.), *Cooperation and Competition Among Primitive Peoples*. New York: McGraw-Hill.

_____. 1938. *The Ojibwa Woman*. Columbia University Contributions to Anthropology 31. New York: Columbia University Press.

Lett, J. 1987. *The Human Enterprise*. Boulder, CO: Westview Press.

Lewis, D. 1973. "Anthropology and Colonialism." *Current Anthropology* 14: 581–602.

Lewis, O. 1951. *Life in a Mexican Village*. Urbana: Univeristy of Illinois Press.

Lowie, R. 1961. *Primitive Society*. New York: Harper and Brothers.

Malinowski, B. 1970. "Practical Anthropology." In J.A. Clifton (ed.), *Applied Anthropology*. (First published 1929.) Boston: Houghton Mifflin.

Manyoni, J.R. 1983. "Eager Visitor, Reluctant Host: The Anthropologist as Stranger." *Anthropologica* 25: 221–49.

Marcus, G.E., and M.J. Fischer. 1986. *Anthropology as Cultural Critique*. University of Chicago Press.

McMillan, A.D. 1988. *Native Peoples and Cultures of Canada*. Vancouver: Douglas and McIntyre.

Mead, Margaret. 1977. *Letters from the Field: 1925–1975*. New York: Harper.

Nash, D. 1963. "The Ethnologist as Stranger: An Essay in the Sociology of Knowledge." *Southwestern Journal of Anthropology* 19: 149–67.

Pelto, P. 1970. *Anthropological Research*. New York: Harper and Row.

Powdermaker, Hortense. 1966. *Stranger and Friend: The Way of an Anthropologist*. New York: W.W. Norton.

Redfield, R. 1930. *Tepoztlan, A Mexican Village*. University of Chicago Press.

Renner, E. 1984. "On Geertz's Interpretive Theoretical Program." *Current Anthropology* 25 (4): 538–40.

Richer, S. 1988. "Fieldwork and the Commodification of Culture: Why the Natives are Restless." *The Canadian Review of Sociology and Anthropology* 25 (3): 406–20.

Ridington, R. 1988. "Knowledge, Power and the Individual in Subarctic Hunting Societies." *American Anthropologist* 90 (1): 98–110.

_____. 1990. *Little Bit Know Something: Stories in a Language of Anthropology*. Vancouver: Douglas and McIntyre.

Rogers, E.S. 1962. *The Round Lake Ojibwa*. Toronto: Royal Ontario Museum.

Rogers, E.S., and J. Garth Taylor. 1981. "Northern Ojibwa." In *Subarctic*, edited by June Helm, volume 6 of *Handbook of North American Indians*. Washington, DC: Smithsonian Institution.

Ross, Rupert. 1992. *Dancing with a Ghost: Exploring Indian Reality*. Markham, ON: Octopus Publishing Group.

Salisbury, Richard F. 1962. *From Stone to Steel: Economic Consequences of a Technological Change in New Guinea.* Cambridge: Cambridge University Press.

_____. 1986. *A Homeland for the Cree: Regional Development in James Bay 1971–1981.* Montreal: McGill-Queen's University Press.

Scholte, B. 1972. "Toward a Reflexive and Critical Anthropology." In D. Hymes (ed.), *Reinventing Anthropology.* New York: Pantheon Books.

Shankman, P. 1984. "The Thick and the Thin: On the Interpretive Theoretical Program of Clifford Geertz." *Current Anthropology* 25: 261–79.

Spencer, J. 1989. "Anthropology as a Kind of Writing." *Man* 24 (1): 145–64.

Stephenson, P.H. 1993. "On Crossing Borders and Boundaries: A Parallax View of the Postmodern Experience." *Culture* XIII (1): 59–62.

Stymeist, D.H. 1975. *Ethnics and Indians: Social Relations in a Northwestern Ontario Town.* Toronto: Peter Martin Associates.

Szathmary, E.J.E., et al. 1987. "Dietary Change and Plasma Glucose Levels in an Amerindian Population Undergoing Cultural Transition." *Social Science and Medicine* 24: 791–804.

Tanner, A. 1979. *Bringing Home Animals: Religious Ideology and Mode of Production of the Mistassini Cree Hunters.* St. John's: Memorial University of Newfoundland.

Ulin, R.C. 1984. *Understanding Cultures.* Austin: University of Texas Press.

Ward, Martha C. 1989. *Nest in the Wind: Adventures in Anthropology on a Tropical Island.* Prospect Heights, IL: Waveland Press.

Wax, R. 1971. *Doing Fieldwork: Warnings and Advice.* University of Chicago Press.

Weber, Max. 1949. *The Methodology of the Social Sciences.* Glencoe, IL: The Free Press.

Werner, D. 1990. *Amazon Journey: An Anthropologist's Year among Brazil's Mekranoti Indians.* Englewood Cliffs, NJ: Prentice Hall.

Winch, Peter. 1958. *The Idea of a Social Science and its Relation to Philosophy.* London: Routledge and Kegan Paul.